THE LESSONS
OF OCTOBER

LEON TROTSKY

THE LESSONS OF OCTOBER

Centenary Edition

with an introduction by
Duncan Hallas

translation by
John G. Wright

Haymarket Books
Chicago, Illinois

© 2017 Mary Ellen O'Boyle Vanzler

First published in Russian in 1924; translated into English 1925.
Previously published in 1987 by Bookmarks.

This edition published in 2017 by
Haymarket Books
P.O. Box 180165
Chicago, IL 60618
773-583-7884
www.haymarketbooks.org
info@haymarketbooks.org

ISBN: 978-1-60846-738-9

Trade distribution:
In the US, Consortium Book Sales and Distribution, www.cbsd.com
In Canada, Publishers Group Canada, www.pgcbooks.ca
In the UK, Turnaround Publisher Services, www.turnaround-uk.com
All other countries, Publishers Group Worldwide, www.pgw.com

This book was published with the generous support
of Lannan Foundation and Wallace Action Fund.

Cover and text design by Eric Kerl.
Cover art: *Space Force Construction*, by Liubov Popova, 1921.

Library of Congress Cataloging-in-Publication data is available.

Contents

Leon Trotsky (1879–1940) was chairman of the Military Revolutionary Committee which planned and carried out the insurrection of October 1917 in Petrograd. As a leading member of the Bolshevik Party and the Petrograd Soviet, he took part in all the debates about the revolution both before and after October. After the death of Lenin in 1924 Trotsky was leader of the Left Opposition. He was forced into exile from Russia by Stalin in 1929 and assassinated in Mexico in 1940 by one of Stalin's agents.

The Lessons of October first appeared as the preface to a collection of Trotsky's speeches and writings during the year 1917 which was published in autumn 1924 by the Russian state publishing house. It appeared in English the following year.

Duncan Hallas (1925–2002) was a member of the Socialist Workers Party in Britain. He is the author of *Trotsky's Marxism* (Bookmarks 1979) and *The Comintern* (Bookmarks 1985).

Introduction

Duncan Hallas

LEON TROTSKY wrote *The Lessons of October* in September 1924 as a preface to the third volume of his *Collected Works*, a volume of his writings from the year 1917 which was never translated into English. The preface was in fact published separately, before the appearance of the book, in late October 1924. According to the historian E H Carr: '. . . the edition of 5,000 copies was quickly sold out and, when the discussion was at its height, was virtually unobtainable; this led to rumours that it was officially banned.'[1]

'Discussion' is hardly the word. The reaction in the USSR to this short booklet was a storm of polemic, scholastic quibbling, vulgar abuse and down-right falsification. 'Throughout the autumn and winter,' wrote Isaac Deutscher, 'the country's political life was entirely overshadowed by this controversy, which has entered the Bolshevik annals under the odd name of "the literary debate".'[2] Although most forms of *soviet* and party democracy still remained in 1924, Russia was by then ruled in reality by the triumvirate of Zinoviev, Kamenev and Stalin. They had emerged as the ruling group at the twelfth party congress in April 1923 and had consolidated their position in the anti-Trotsky campaign of December 1923, the party conference of January 1924 and the thirteenth party congress of May 1924. Much later Trotsky, writing in exile in 1933, was to describe the twelfth congress as the last genuine congress of the Russian Communist Party, the later ones being mere 'bureaucratic charades'. The anti-Trotsky campaign was the last occasion on which the speeches and writings of opponents of the dominant group appeared undistorted in the party press.

Yet Trotsky, although powerless in fact, was still a member of the ruling politbureau and, as Commissar for War, of the Soviet government. His prestige stood high in the international communist movement, the more so since the death of Lenin in January 1924 after a long illness left him the best-known surviving leader of 1917. In 1924 this still counted for something. This in part accounted for the virulence of the attacks made on him in the 'literary debate'; but there was another factor.

Stalin, Kamenev and Zinoviev had in common the fact that they were 'old Bolsheviks'. Kamenev and Zinoviev had been members of the Bolshevik fraction from its beginning in 1903, Stalin from 1904. All three had been members of the first purely Bolshevik central committee after the final split with the Mensheviks in 1912, Zinoviev by election at the Bolshevik Prague Conference, Stalin and Kamenev by subsequent co-option. Zinoviev had been Lenin's companion in exile from 1908 till 1917, had been co-author with Lenin of *Socialism and War* (1915), the definitive Bolshevik statement on the imperialist war and the collapse of the Second

International. He had been an intransigent supporter of Lenin at the conferences of Zimmerwald and Kienthal when the anti-war policy had been hammered out. Since 1919 he had been president of the Communist International. Kamenev too had shared Lenin's exile till 1914, when he was sent back to Russia. Stalin, less close personally to Lenin, had nevertheless been a professional party revolutionary throughout the pre-revolutionary period. He had written, with Lenin's help, an important book on the Bolshevik attitude to the national question, and had been, since April 1922, general secretary of the party.

All three had been actively promoting a cult of 'Leninism' since Lenin had become incapacitated (he suffered a paralysing stroke in May 1922 and two further strokes near the end of the year; by March 1923 his political life was over, though he lived on paralysed until January 1924). Leaving aside for the moment the underlying political content of this cult, entirely alien to the spirit of Lenin's own attitudes as it was, its immediate function was obvious. The triumvirate represented themselves as proven pillars of Bolshevik orthodoxy, faithful disciples of the infallible Lenin—as he was now being represented—whereas Trotsky, as was well known, had frequently opposed Lenin in the past and had not joined the Bolshevik Party until the summer of 1917.

The Lessons of October struck a most damaging blow both at the myths of the immaculate conception and seamless perfection of Bolshevism and at the political record of the triumvirs themselves, above all at their record in the crucial year 1917.

'We have already said, and we repeat, that the study of disagreements cannot, and ought not in any case, be regarded as an attack against those comrades who followed a false policy. But on the other hand, it is absolutely impermissible to blot out the greatest chapter in the history of our party merely because some party members failed to keep step with the proletarian revolution,' says the text, '. . . even within this party, among its tops, on the eve of decisive action there was formed a group of experienced revolutionaries, old Bolsheviks who were in sharp opposition to the proletarian revolution; and who, in the most critical period of the revolution from February 1917 to approximately February 1918, adopted on all the fundamental questions an essentially social-democratic position. It needed Lenin, and Lenin's exceptional influence in the party . . . to safeguard the party and the revolution against the supreme confusion following from such a condition.'

'These comrades', 'some comrades'. . . they included, most conspicuously, and in varying degrees, Zinoviev, Kamenev and Stalin. Inevitably in the circumstances, they most certainly regarded *The Lessons of October* as a direct attack on themselves.

Consider the indictment. Soon after the February revolution and the overthrow of the Tsar, the Bolshevik paper *Pravda* adopted a 'defencist' attitude, offering critical support for the war 'in defence of the revolution'. This was similar to the attitude which Lenin had so furiously denounced when it was advanced by the French and German 'lefts'. *Pravda*'s general position can be fairly described as one of critical support for the Provisional Government. Pre-eminent among

those responsible for this line were the two central committee members who had been able to return from Siberian exile
to Petrograd in March 1917: Kamenev and Stalin.

When Lenin returned to Russia in April, determined
to transform the party's line to 'Down with the Provisional
Government, Down with the War' and to win the party to
the *perspective* of workers' power, the proletarian revolution,
he was opposed by the 'old Bolsheviks' led by Kamenev. They
clung to Lenin's own previous slogan, calling for the 'democratic (in other words, *bourgeois*) dictatorship of the proletariat and peasantry', a position Lenin himself now described as
'antiquated . . . worthless . . . dead'.

Most damaging of all, Zinoviev and Kamenev (though
not Stalin, who had slid away from his earlier position)
opposed the whole project of the October insurrection—and
not only inside the central committee but *publicly*, an act
denounced by Lenin as 'strike-breaking'.

An objective revolutionary assessment might well agree
with Lenin's own, in his then unpublished 'Testament',
where he writes: '. . . the October episode of Zinoviev and
Kamenev was not, of course, accidental, but . . . it ought to be
as little used against them as the non-Bolshevism of Trotsky.'
Written at the end of 1922, this document ends with a post-
script dated at the beginning of 1923 which calls for Stalin's
removal from the position of party general secretary. Such an
assessment would take into account the *inevitable* element of
conservatism in the party in a new and fast-changing situation in 1917, as Trotsky so cogently argues in *The Lessons of
October*, but it would also consider the inadequacy of Lenin's
own position before April 1917.

An objective revolutionary assessment was, however, the last thing to be expected in the circumstances of late 1924. Instead there was a massive, well-orchestrated and entirely hostile response to *The Lessons of October*. The triumvirate and the apparatus they controlled were concerned above all to preserve their power and their essentially conservative policy. Innumerable articles in the officially-controlled press denounced Trotsky. Replies of any substance were refused publication.

Early in 1925 a massive volume, *On Leninism*, appeared. It contained refutations of Trotsky's *The Lessons of October* and polemics by Andreev, Bukharin, Kamenev, Krupskaya, Molotov, Rykov, Sokolnikov, Stalin, Zinoviev and six others against his political positions since 1903. This work was translated, often in abbreviated form, into the main languages of the Communist International. The English version, published in 1925, was titled *The Errors of Trotskyism*. The apparatus campaign was entirely successful. By December 1924 Stalin, appearing now as an independent theoretician rather than an apparatchik, felt confident enough to proclaim the doctrine, totally foreign to the ideas put forward by Lenin, of 'Socialism in One Country'—and naturally he did this in the name of 'Leninism'.

The outcome of the 'literary debate' proved two things: first that an appeal to reason, Marxism and revolutionary tradition inside the Communist Party of the Soviet Union was hopeless by late 1924; second, that the Communist International itself, and specifically its major parties, was unable to challenge the triumvirate even when its vital interests were involved.

To take this second point first. In 1923 the central committees of the French, German and Polish Communist Parties, at that time among the largest and most promising parties outside the USSR, had protested against the anti-Trotsky campaign. By 1925, however, they had all endorsed *On Leninism* and, still more damaging and ultimately devastating for them, the doctrine of 'Socialism in One Country'. The reasons for this political collapse are varied in their specific details but have a common factor: all three parties failed to meet up to their expectations in the revolutionary or near-revolutionary crisis of 1923; this was true above all of the German party, which was the strongest. This, in the end, is what made them pliable to manipulation from a Moscow centre which was less and less concerned with their independent role and more and more concerned with the impact of their activities on the power struggle inside the USSR and, later, with their utility as pressure points in the diplomacy of the USSR with other states.

The Lessons of October was addressed to the communist *parties*, not simply to the communist party in power in the USSR. Trotsky's argument starts from the need to study the events of *1923* in the light of an unfalsified account of 1917. As he writes: 'Last year we met with two crushing defeats in Bulgaria. First, the party missed an exceptionally favourable moment for revolutionary action . . . then the party, striving to make good its mistake, plunged into the September insurrection without having made the necessary political or organisational preparations. The Bulgarian revolution ought to have been a prelude to the German revolution. Unfortunately the bad Bulgarian prelude led to an even worse sequel in Germany itself. In the latter part of last year, we witnessed in Germany a classic demonstration of how it is possible to miss a perfectly exceptional revolutionary situation of world-historic importance.'

That defeat in Germany was indeed of world-historic importance . . . it led, ultimately though not inevitably, to Hitler and the Second World War. It also led to the consolidation of bureaucratic rule in the USSR and, eventually, to Stalin's dictatorship and the total destruction of the elements of workers' power that then still survived.

Earlier in this introduction the question of what the triumvirate of Stalin, Zinoviev and Kamenev really represented was postponed. It must now be addressed. Isaac Deutscher wrote of the political situation in the year 1921: 'Whom then did the Bolshevik Party represent? It represented only itself, that is, its past association with the working class, its present aspiration to act as the guardian of the proletarian class interest, and its intention to re-assemble in the course of economic reconstruction a new working class which should be able in due time to take the country's destiny into its hands. In the meantime the Bolshevik Party maintained itself in power by usurpation.'[3]

Deutscher writes 'its past association with the working class' for two reasons. First because the working class, as it is sociologically defined, had shrivelled from around three million to around one million in the years of civil war, foreign intervention and devastation from 1918 to 1921. Secondly because the class-conscious minority of this working class, itself a minority within a working population, which was mostly peasants, had either been killed during the civil war, been drawn into administration, or had become demoralised. The peasant masses, having got possession of the land, were now indifferent to the Soviet government, or hostile.

The party in power, therefore, had become 'substitutionalist'. Such a state of affairs can perhaps be 'carried' for a short time without the party itself being transformed—but not for years on end. By 1924, indeed by 1923 if not earlier, this transformation had taken place. Party and state apparatuses were becoming one. Of course this was still far from the Stalinist tyranny of the future, but the party had effectively become an apparatus party by the early 1920s. The mass recruitment, the 'Lenin Levy' decided upon by the thirteenth party conference, inevitably *weakened* the influence of those party members who still had some Marxist training and internationalist ideas. These included, of course, the supporters of Kamenev and Zinoviev, who soon found themselves in opposition to Stalin, the apparatchik-in-chief, and as impotent as Trotsky. Both were later to face trial and execution.

Our knowledge of the outcome of the 'literary debate' in no way reduces the importance of *The Lessons of October*. In this book Trotsky concerns himself with several issues which are alive today.

The whole argument of the book assumes the centrality of the revolutionary socialist party: '. . . events have proved that without a party capable of directing the proletarian revolution, the revolution itself is rendered impossible . . . there is nothing else that can serve the proletariat as a substitute for its own party.' Trotsky does not say that *any* revolution is rendered impossible, for that was proved not so in Russia in February 1917 and has been again many times since, but for the working class to take and hold power the revolutionary party is indispensible.

Trotsky is not concerned here with the problems involved in building such a party, although implicitly some of what he has to say about party conservatism applies to *every* stage of party development from Marxist study circles onwards. His theme, however, is the party in a revolutionary situation, and what he calls 'almost an unalterable law that a party crisis is inevitable in the transition from the preparatory revolutionary activity to the immediate struggle for power.'

There is no need to develop the point here; the whole text is a sermon on this proposition. Three brief comments are enough.

First, Trotsky's explanation of the upsurge of the Social-Revolutionaries after February 1917 (and to a much smaller extent the Mensheviks), while essentially correct, may underestimate the degree to which *any* great revolution, throwing previously passive millions into political life, can temporarily strengthen 'left' and not-so-left reformists and centrists. Many occasions, from Germany 1918–19 to Portugal 1974–75, provide evidence of this. If this is so, it in no way weakens the thrust of Trotsky's argument; rather it strengthens it.

Secondly, the role of a party 'cadre', an experienced layer of party members, apart from the top leadership, is of decisive importance in executing sharp turns in policy. Lenin, returning in April 1917 with his theses, would not have been able to shift the political line of the Bolshevik Party alone. There had to be a layer of politically experienced party members who could respond to the arguments, and respond quickly. Such a cadre cannot be improvised. It has to be built and tested in the 'preparatory' years when revolutionary change is not on the agenda.

Finally, without the concrete and essentially correct analyses made by Lenin during these years, and by Trotsky himself too in 1917, without the ability to judge what was still vital and what must be corrected, and do all this in time, the October revolution would not have succeeded.

Duncan Hallas
July 1987

A rising of the masses of the people needs no justification. What has happened is an insurrection, and not a conspiracy. We hardened the revolutionary energy of the Petersburg workers and soldiers. We openly forged the will of the masses for an insurrection, and not a conspiracy. The masses of the people followed our banner and our insurrection was victorious.

And now we are told: renounce your victory, make concessions, compromise. With whom? I ask: with whom ought we to compromise? With those wretched groups who have left us or who are making this proposal?

But after all we've had a full view of them. No one in Russia is with them any longer. A compromise is supposed to be made, as between two equal sides, by the millions of workers and peasants represented in this Congress, whom they are ready, not for the first time or the last, to barter away as the bourgeoisie sees fit.

No, here no compromise is possible. To those who have left and to those who tell us to do this we must say: you are miserable bankrupts, your role is played out; go where you ought to be: into the dustbin of history!

Leon Trotsky,
speaking to the All-Russian Congress of Soviets on the morning after the October insurrection

Chapter One
We must study
the October revolution

WE MET with success in the October Revolution, but the October Revolution has met with little success in our press. Up to the present time we lack a single work which gives a comprehensive picture of the October upheaval and puts the proper stress upon its most important political and organizational aspects.* Worse yet, even the available firsthand material—including the most important documents—directly pertaining to the various particulars of the preparation for the revolution, or the revolution itself, remains unpublished as yet. Numerous documents and considerable material have been issued bearing on the pre-October history of the revolution and the pre-October history of the party; we have also issued much material and many documents relating to the post-October period. But October itself has received far less

---

*   This essay was written in Russia in September 1924. Trotsky's own *History of the Russian Revolution* was not to be published until 1932, when he was in exile.

attention. Having achieved the revolution, we seem to have concluded that we should never have to repeat it. It is as if we thought that no immediate and direct benefit for the unpostponable tasks of future constructive work could be derived from the study of October; the actual conditions of the direct preparation for it; the actual accomplishment of it; and the work of consolidating it during the first few weeks.

Such an approach—though it may be subconscious—is, however, profoundly erroneous, and is, moreover, narrow and nationalistic. We ourselves may never have to repeat the experience of the October Revolution, but this does not at all imply that we have nothing to learn from that experience. We are a part of the International,* and the workers in all other countries are still faced with the solution of the problem of their own 'October'. Last year we had ample proof that the most advanced Communist parties of the West had not only failed to assimilate our October experience but were virtually ignorant of the actual facts.**

To be sure, the objection may be raised that it is impossible to study October or even to publish documents relating to October without the risk of stirring up old disagreements. But such an approach to the question would be altogether petty. The disagreements of 1917 were indeed very profound, and they were not by any means accidental. But nothing could be more paltry than an attempt to turn them now, after a lapse of several years, into weapons of attack

---

*   The Third or Communist International, also known as the Comintern.

** For a brief account of the events of 1923, see Appendix 2 below.

against those who were at that time mistaken. It would be, however, even more inadmissible to remain silent as regards the most important problems of the October Revolution, which are of international significance, on account of trifling personal considerations.

Last year we met with two crushing defeats in Bulgaria. First, the party let slip an exceptionally favourable moment for revolutionary action on account of fatalistic and doctrinaire considerations. (That moment was the rising of the peasants after the June coup of Tsankov.) Then the party, striving to make good its mistake, plunged into the September insurrection without having made the necessary political or organizational preparations. The Bulgarian revolution ought to have been a prelude to the German revolution. Unfortunately, the bad Bulgarian prelude led to an even worse sequel in Germany itself. In the latter part of last year, we witnessed in Germany a classic demonstration of how it is possible to miss a perfectly exceptional revolutionary situation of world-historic importance. Once more, however, neither the Bulgarian nor even the German experiences of last year have received an adequate or sufficiently concrete appraisal. The author of these lines drew a general outline of the development of events in Germany last year. Everything that transpired since then has borne out this outline in part and as a whole. No one else has even attempted to advance any other explanation. But we need more than an outline. It is indispensable for us to have a concrete account, full of factual data, of last year's developments in Germany. What we need is such an account as would provide a concrete explanation of the causes of this most cruel historic defeat.

It is difficult, however, to speak of an analysis of the events in Bulgaria and Germany when we have not, up to the present, given a politically and tactically elaborated account of the October Revolution. We have never made clear to ourselves what we accomplished and how we accomplished it. After October, in the flush of victory, it seemed as if the events of Europe would develop of their own accord and, moreover, within so brief a period as would leave no time for any theoretical assimilation of the lessons of October.

But the events have proved that without a party capable of directing the proletarian revolution, the revolution itself is rendered impossible. The proletariat cannot seize power by a spontaneous uprising. Even in highly industrialized and highly cultured Germany the spontaneous uprising of the toilers—in November 1918—only succeeded in transferring power to the hands of the bourgeoisie. One propertied class is able to seize the power that has been wrested from another propertied class because it is able to base itself upon its riches, its cultural level, and its innumerable connections with the old state apparatus. But there is nothing else that can serve the proletariat as a substitute for its own party.

It was only by the middle of 1921 that the fully rounded-out work of building the Communist parties really began (under the slogan 'Win the masses', 'United front', etc.). The problems of October receded and, simultaneously, the study of October was also relegated to the background. Last year we found ourselves once again face to face with the problems of the proletarian revolution. It is high time we collected all documents, printed all available material, and applied ourselves to their study!

We are well aware, of course, that every nation, every class, and even every party learns primarily from the harsh blows of its own experience. But that does not in the least imply that the experience of other countries and classes and parties is of minor importance. Had we failed to study the Great French Revolution, the revolution of 1848, and the Paris Commune, we should never have been able to achieve the October Revolution, even though we passed through the experience of the year 1905. And after all, we went through this 'national' experience of ours basing ourselves on deductions from previous revolutions, and extending their historical line. Afterwards, the entire period of the counter-revolution was taken up with the study of the lessons to be learned and the deductions to be drawn from the year 1905.

Yet no such work has been done with regard to the victorious revolution of 1917—no, not even a tenth part of it. Of course we are not now living through the years of reaction, nor are we in exile. On the other hand, the forces and resources at our command now are in no way comparable to what we had during those years of hardship. All that we need do is to pose clearly and plainly the task of studying the October Revolution, both on the party scale and on the scale of the International as a whole. It is indispensable for the entire party, and especially its younger generations, to study and assimilate step by step the experience of October, which provided the supreme, incontestable, and irrevocable test of the past and opened wide the gates to the future. The

German lesson of last year is not only a serious reminder but also a dire warning.

An objection will no doubt be raised that even the most thorough knowledge of the course of the October Revolution would by no means have guaranteed victory to our German party. But this kind of wholesale and essentially philistine rationalizing will get us nowhere. To be sure, mere study of the October Revolution is not sufficient to secure victory in other countries; but circumstances may arise where all the prerequisites for revolution exist, with the exception of a far-seeing and resolute party leadership grounded in the understanding of the laws and methods of the revolution. This was exactly the situation last year in Germany. Similar situations may recur in other countries. But for the study of the laws and methods of proletarian revolution there is, up to the present time, no more important and profound a source than our October experience. Leaders of European Communist parties who fail to assimilate the history of October by means of a critical and closely detailed study would resemble a commander in chief preparing new wars under modern conditions, who fails to study the strategic, tactical, and technical experience of the last imperialist war. Such a commander in chief would inevitably doom his armies to defeat in the future.

The fundamental instrument of proletarian revolution is the party. On the basis of our experience—even taking only one year, from February 1917 to February 1918—and on the basis of the supplementary experience in Finland, Hungary, Italy, Bulgaria, and Germany, we can posit as almost an unalterable law that a party crisis is inevitable in the transition from preparatory revolutionary activity to the immediate struggle for power. Generally speaking, crises arise in the party at every serious turn in the party's course, either as a prelude to the turn or as a consequence of it. The explanation for this lies in the fact that every period in the development of the party has special features of its own and calls for specific habits and methods of work. A tactical turn implies a greater or lesser break in these habits and methods. Herein lies the direct and most immediate root of internal party frictions and crises.

'Too often has it happened,' wrote Lenin in July 1917, 'that, when history has taken a sharp turn, even progressive parties have for some time been unable to adapt themselves to the new situation and have repeated slogans which had formerly been correct but had now lost all meaning—lost it as "suddenly" as the sharp turn in history was "sudden".'[1] Hence the danger arises that if the turn is too abrupt or too sudden, and if in the preceding period too many elements of inertia and conservatism have accumulated in the leading organs of the party, then the party will prove itself unable to fulfill its leadership at that supreme and critical moment for which it has been preparing itself in the course of years or decades. The party is ravaged by a crisis, and the movement passes the party by—and heads toward defeat.

A revolutionary party is subjected to the pressure of other political forces. At every given stage of its development the party elaborates its own methods of counteracting and resisting this pressure. During a tactical turn and the resulting internal regroupments and frictions, the party's power of resistance becomes weakened. From this the possibility always arises that the internal groupings in the party, which originate from the necessity of a turn in tactics, may develop far beyond the original controversial points of departure and serve as a support for various class tendencies. To put the case more plainly: the party that does not keep step with the historical tasks of its own class becomes, or runs the risk of becoming, the indirect tool of other classes.

If what we said above is true of every serious turn in tactics, it is all the more true of great turns in strategy. By tactics in politics we understand, using the analogy of military science, the art of conducting isolated operations. By strategy, we understand the art of conquest, i.e., the seizure of power. Prior to the war we did not, as a rule, make this distinction. In the epoch of the Second International we confined ourselves solely to the conception of social democratic tactics. Nor was this accidental. The social democracy applied parliamentary tactics, trade union tactics, municipal tactics, cooperative tactics, and so on. But the question of combining all forces and resources—all sorts of troops—to obtain victory over the enemy was really never raised in the epoch of the Second International, insofar as the practical task of the struggle for power was not raised. It was only the 1905 revolution that first posed, after a long interval, the fundamental or strategical questions of proletarian struggle. By reason of this it secured immense advantages to the revolutionary Russian social democrats, i.e., the Bolsheviks. The great epoch of revolutionary strategy began in 1917, first for Russia and afterwards for the rest of Europe. Strategy, of course, does not do away with tactics. The questions of the trade union movement, of parliamentary activity, and so on, do not disappear, but they now become invested with a new meaning as subordinate methods of a combined struggle for power. Tactics are subordinated to strategy.

If tactical turns usually lead to internal friction in the party, how much deeper and fiercer must be the friction resulting from strategical turns! And the most abrupt of all turns is the turn of the proletarian party from the work of preparation and propaganda, or organization and agitation, to the immediate struggle for power, to an armed insurrection against the bourgeoisie. Whatever remains in the party that is irresolute, skeptical, conciliationist, capitulatory—in short, Menshevik—all this rises to the surface in opposition to the insurrection, seeks theoretical formulas to justify its opposition, and finds them ready-made in the arsenal of the opportunist opponents of yesterday. We shall have occasion to observe this phenomenon more than once in the future.

The final review and selection of party weapons on the eve of the decisive struggle took place during the interval from February to October [1917] on the basis of the widest possible agitational and organizational work among the masses. During and after October these weapons were tested in the fire of colossal historic actions. To undertake at the present time, several years after October, an appraisal of the different viewpoints concerning revolution in general, and the Russian revolution in particular, and in so doing to evade the experience of 1917, is to busy oneself with barren scholasticism. That would certainly not be a Marxist political analysis. It would be analogous to wrangling over the advantages of various sytems of swimming while we stubbornly refused to turn our eyes to the river where swimmers were putting these systems into practice. No better test of viewpoints concerning revolution exists than the verification of how they worked out during the revolution itself, just as a system of swimming is best tested when a swimmer jumps into the water.

Chapter Two
'The democratic dictatorship of the proletariat and the peasantry'— in February and October

THE COURSE and the outcome of the October Revolution dealt a relentless blow to the scholastic parody of Marxism which was very widespread among the Russian social democrats, beginning in part with the Emancipation of Labor Group* and finding its most finished expression among the Mensheviks. The essence of this pseudo-Marxism consisted in perverting Marx's conditional and limited conception that 'the country that is more developed industrially only shows, to the less developed, the image of its own future' into an absolute and (to use Marx's own expression) suprahistorical law; and then, in seeking to establish upon the basis of that law the tactics of the proletarian party. Such a formulation

---

* The group was founded by Plekhanov and other Russian emigres in Switzerland in 1883.

naturally excluded even the mention of any struggle on the part of the Russian proletariat for the seizure of power until the more highly developed countries had set a 'precedent'.

There is, of course, no disputing that every backward country finds *some* traits of its own future in the history of advanced countries, but there cannot be any talk of a repetition of the development as a whole. On the contrary, the more capitalist economy acquired a world character, all the more strikingly original became the development of the backward countries, which had to necessarily combine elements of their backwardness with the latest achievements of capitalist development. In his preface to *The Peasant War in Germany*, Engels wrote: 'At a certain point, which must not necessarily appear simultaneously and on the same stage of development everywhere, [the bourgeoisie] begins to note that this, its second self [the proletariat] has outgrown it'.[2]

The course of historical development constrained the Russian bourgeoisie to make this observation much earlier and more completely than the bourgeoisie of all other countries. Lenin, even prior to 1905, gave expression to the peculiar character of the Russian revolution in the formula 'the democratic dictatorship of the proletariat and the peasantry'. This formula, in itself, as future development showed, could acquire meaning only as a stage toward the socialist dictatorship of the proletariat supported by the peasantry. Lenin's formulation of the problem, revolutionary and dynamic through and through, was completely and irreconcilably counterposed to the Menshevik pattern, according to which Russia could pretend only to a repetition of the history of the advanced nations, with the bourgeoisie in power and the social democrats in opposition.

Some circles of our party, however, laid the stress not upon the *dictatorship* of the proletariat and the peasantry in Lenin's formula, but upon its *democratic* character as opposed to its socialist character. And, again, this could only mean that in Russia, a backward country, only a democratic revolution was conceivable. The socialist revolution was to begin in the West; and we could take to the road of socialism only in the wake of England, France, and Germany. But such a formulation of the question slipped inevitably into Menshevism, and this was fully revealed in 1917 when the tasks of the revolution were posed before us, not for prognosis but for decisive action.

Under the actual conditions of revolution, to hold a position of supporting democracy, pushed to its logical conclusion—*opposing* socialism as *'being premature'*—meant, in politics, to shift from a proletarian to a petty-bourgeois position. It meant going over to the position of the left wing of national revolution.

The February revolution, if considered by itself, was a bourgeois revolution.* But as a bourgeois revolution it came too late and was devoid of any stability. Torn asunder by contradictions which immediately found their expression in dual power, it had to either change into a direct prelude to the proletarian revolution—which is what actually did happen— or throw Russia back into a semicolonial existence, under some sort of bourgeois-oligarchic regime. Consequently, the period following the February revolution could be regarded

---

* For a brief outline of the events of 1917, see Appendix 1 below.

from two points of view: either as a period of consolidating, developing, or consummating the 'democratic' revolution, or as a period of preparation for the proletarian revolution. The first point of view was held not only by the Mensheviks and the Social Revolutionaries [SRS] but also by a certain section of our own party leadership, with this difference that the latter really tried to push democratic revolution as far as possible to the left. But the method was essentially one and the same—to 'exert pressure' on the ruling bourgeoisie, a 'pressure' so calculated as to remain within the framework of the bourgeois democratic regime. If that policy had prevailed, the development of the revolution would have passed over the head of our party, and in the end the insurrection of the worker and peasant masses would have taken place without party leadership, in other words, we would have had a repetition of the July days* on a colossal scale, i.e., this time not as an episode but as a catastrophe.

It is perfectly obvious that the immediate consequence of such a catastrophe would have been the physical destruction of our party. This provides us with a measuring stick of how deep our differences of opinion were.

---

*   The July Days of 1917 saw mass spontaneous demonstrations of armed workers and soldiers demanding an end to the Provisional Government and 'All power to the *soviets!*' As a revolutionary movement it was premature. The leadership of the *soviets* had no intention of breaking with the Provisional Government. It was followed by a period of reaction and a witch-hunt against the Bolsheviks. See Tony Cliff, *Lenin 1914–1917: All power to the Soviets* (Bookmarks, London 1985) pages 258–272.

The influence of the Mensheviks and the sRs in the first period of the revolution was not, of course, accidental. It reflected the preponderance of petty-bourgeois masses—mainly peasants—in the population, and the immaturity of the revolution itself. It was precisely that immaturity, amidst the extremely exceptional circumstances arising from the war, which placed in the hands of the petty-bourgeois revolutionists the leadership, or at least the semblance of leadership, which came to this: that they defended the historical rights of the bourgeoisie to power. But this does not in the least mean that the Russian revolution could have taken no course other than the one it did from February to October 1917. The latter course flowed not only from the relations between the classes but also from the temporary circumstances created by the war. Because of the war, the peasantry was organized and armed in an army of many millions. Before the proletariat succeeded in organizing itself under its own banner and taking the leadership of the rural masses, the petty-bourgeois revolutionists found a natural support in the peasant army, which was rebelling against the war. By the ponderous weight of this multimillioned army upon which, after all, everything directly depended, the petty-bourgeois revolutionists brought pressure to bear on the workers and carried them along in the first period.

That the revolution might have taken a different course on the same class foundations is best of all demonstrated by the events immediately preceding the war. In July 1914 Petrograd was convulsed by revolutionary strikes. Matters had gone so far as open fighting in the streets. The absolute leadership of that movement was in the hands of the underground organization and the legal press of our party. Bolshevism was increasing its influence in a direct struggle against liquidationism and the petty-bourgeois parties generally. The further growth of the movement would have meant above all the growth of the Bolshevik Party. The *soviets* of workers' deputies in 1914—if developments had reached the stage of *soviets*—would probably have been Bolshevik from the outset. The awakening of the villages would have proceeded under the direct or indirect leadership of the city *soviets*, led by the Bolsheviks. This does not necessarily mean that the SRS would have immediately disappeared from the villages. No. In all probability the first stage of the peasant revolution would have occurred under the banner of the Narodniks [populists]. But with a development of events such as we have sketched, the Narodniks themselves would have been compelled to push their left wing to the fore, in order to seek an alliance with the Bolshevik *soviets* in the cities.

Of course, the immediate outcome of the insurrection would have depended, even in such a case, in the first instance upon the mood and conduct of the army, which was bound up with the peasantry. It is impossible and even superfluous to guess now whether the movement of 1914–15 would have led to victory had not the outbreak of the war forged a new and gigantic link in the chain of developments. Considerable evidence, however, may be adduced that had the victorious revolution unfolded along the course which began with the events in July 1914, the overthrow of the tsarist monarchy would, in all likelihood, have meant the immediate assumption of power by the revolutionary workers' *soviets*, and the latter, through the medium of the left Narodniks, would (from the very outset!) have drawn the peasant masses within their orbit.

The war interrupted the unfolding revolutionary movement. It acted at first to retard but afterwards to accelerate it enormously. Through the medium of the multimillioned army, the war created an absolutely exceptional base, both socially and organizationally, for the petty-bourgeois parties. For the peculiarity of the peasantry consists precisely in the fact that despite their great numbers it is difficult to form the peasants into an organized base, even when they are imbued with a revolutionary spirit. Hoisting themselves on the shoulders of a ready-made organization, that is, the army, the petty-bourgeois parties overawed the proletariat and befogged it with defensism.*

That is why Lenin at once came out furiously against the old slogan of 'the democratic dictatorship of the proletariat and the peasantry', which under the new circumstances meant the transformation of the Bolshevik Party into the left wing of the defensist bloc. For Lenin the main task was to lead the proletarian vanguard from the swamp of defensism out into the clear. Only on that condition could the proletariat at the next stage become the axis around which the toiling masses of the village would group themselves. But in

---

* That is, they called for support for the Provisional Government in continuing the war against Germany 'in defence of the revolution'. After February 1917 this was also the position taken by a large part of the Bolshevik Party, including *Pravda*, of which Stalin was one of the editors. Lenin, on the other hand, argued that the war remained an imperialist war, waged by a bourgeois Provisional Government. He continued to argue for revolutionary defeatism.

that case what should our attitude be toward the democratic revolution, or rather toward the democratic dictatorship of the old proletariat and the peasantry? Lenin was ruthless in refuting the 'Old Bolsheviks' who 'more than once already have played so regrettable a role in the history of our Party by reiterating formulas senselessly *learned by rote* instead of *studying* the specific features of the new and living reality . . . But one must measure up not to old formulas but to the new reality. Is this reality covered by Comrade Kamenev's Old Bolshevik formula, which says that "the bourgeois democratic revolution is not completed"?

'It is not,' Lenin answers. 'The formula is obsolete. It is no good at all. It is dead. And it is no use trying to revive it.'[3]

To be sure, Lenin occasionally remarked that the *soviets* of workers', soldiers', and peasants' deputies in the first period of the February revolution did, *to a certain degree*, embody the revolutionary democratic dictatorship of the proletariat and the peasantry. And this was true insofar as these *soviets* embodied power in general. But, as Lenin time and again explained, the *soviets* of the February period embodied only demi-power. They supported the power of the bourgeoisie while exercising semi-oppositionist 'pressure' upon it. And it was precisely this intermediate position that did not permit them to transcend the framework of the democratic coalition of workers, peasants, and soldiers. In its form of rule, this coalition tended toward dictatorship to the extent that it did not rely upon regulated governmental relations but upon armed force and direct revolutionary supervision. However, it fell far short of an actual dictatorship.

The instability of the conciliationist *soviets* lay precisely in this democratic amorphousness of a demi-power coalition of workers, peasants, and soldiers. The *soviets* had to either disappear entirely or take real power into their hands. But they could take power not in the capacity of a democratic coalition of workers and peasants represented by different parties, but only as the dictatorship of the proletariat directed by a single party and drawing after it the peasant masses, beginning with their semi-proletarian sections. In other words, a democratic workers' and peasants' coalition could only take shape as an immature form of power incapable of attaining real power—it could take shape only as a tendency and not as a concrete fact. Any further movement toward the attainment of power inevitably had to explode the democratic shell, confront the majority of the peasantry with the necessity of following the workers, provide the proletariat with an opportunity to realize a class dictatorship, and thereby place on the agenda—along with a complete and ruthlessly radical democratization of social relations—a purely socialist invasion of the workers' state into the sphere of capitalist property rights. Under such circumstances, whoever continued to cling to the formula of a 'democratic dictatorship' in effect renounced power and led the revolution into a blind alley.

The fundamental controversial question around which everything else centred was this: whether or not we should struggle for power; whether or not we should assume power. This alone is ample proof that we were not then dealing with a mere episodic difference of opinion but with two tendencies of the utmost principled significance. The first and principled tendency was proletarian and led to the road of world revolution. The other was 'democratic', i.e. petty bourgeois, and led, in the last instance, to the subordination of proletarian policies to the requirements of bourgeois society in the process of reform. These two tendencies came into hostile conflict over every essential question that arose throughout the year 1917. It is precisely the revolutionary epoch—i.e., the epoch when the accumulated capital of the party is put in direct circulation—that must inevitably broach in action and reveal divergences of such a nature.

These two tendencies, in greater or lesser degree, with more or less modification, will more than once manifest themselves during the revolutionary period in every country. If by Bolshevism—and we are stressing here its essential aspect—we understand such training, tempering, and organization of the proletarian vanguard as enables the latter to seize power, arms in hand; and if by social democracy we are to understand the acceptance of reformist oppositional activity within the framework of bourgeois society and an adaptation to its legality—i.e., the actual training of the masses to become imbued with the inviolability of the bourgeois state; then, indeed, it is absolutely clear that even within the Communist Party itself, which does not emerge full-fledged from the crucible of history, the struggle between social democratic tendencies and Bolshevism is bound to reveal itself in its most clear, open and un-camouflaged form during the immediate revolutionary period when the question of power is raised point-blank.

The problem of the conquest of power was put before the party only after 4 April, that is, after the arrival of Lenin in Petrograd. But even after that moment, the political line of the party did not by any means acquire a unified and indivisible character, challenged by none. Despite the decisions of the April Conference in 1917, the opposition to the revolutionary course—sometimes hidden, sometimes open—pervaded the entire period of preparation.

The study of the trend of the disagreements between February and the consolidation of the October Revolution is not only of extraordinary theoretical importance, but of the utmost practical importance. In 1910 Lenin spoke of the disagreements at the Second Party Congress in 1903 as 'anticipatory', i.e., a forewarning. It is very important to trace these disagreements to their source, i.e., 1903, or even at an earlier time, say beginning with 'Economism'.* But such a study acquires meaning only if it is carried to its logical conclusion and if it covers the period in which these disagreements were submitted to the decisive test, that is to say, the October period.

We cannot, within the limits of this preface, undertake to deal exhautively with all the stages of this struggle. But we consider it indispensable at least partially to fill up the deplorable gap in our literature with regard to the most important period in the development of our party.

As has already been said, the disagreements centred around the question of power. Generally speaking, this is the

---

* The Economists held that the economic struggle of the working class was in itself sufficient to develop a mass movement and revolutionary leadership. They therefore played down the importance of the revolutionary party.

touchstone whereby the character of the revolutionary party (and of other parties as well) is determined.

There is an intimate connection between the question of power and the question of war which was posed and decided in this period. We propose to consider these questions in chronological order, taking the outstanding landmarks: the position of the party and of the party press in the first period after the overthrow of tsarism and prior to the arrival of Lenin; the struggle around Lenin's theses; the April Conference; the aftermath of the July days; the Kornilov period; the Democratic Conference and the Pre-Parliament; the question of the armed insurrection and seizure of power (September to October); and the question of a 'homogeneous' socialist government.

The study of these disagreements will, we believe, enable us to draw deductions of considerable importance to other parties in the Communist International.

Chapter Three
The struggle against war and defencism

THE OVERTHROW of tsarism in February 1917 signaled, of course, a gigantic leap forward. But if we take February within the limits of February alone, i.e., if we take it not as a step towards October, then it meant no more than this: that Russia was approximating a bourgeois republic like, for example, France. The petty-bourgeois revolutionary parties, as is their wont, considered the February revolution to be neither bourgeois nor a step toward a socialist revolution, but as some sort of self-sufficing 'democratic' entity. And upon this they constructed the ideology of revolutionary defensism. They were defending, if you please, not the rule of any one class but 'revolution' and 'democracy'. But even in our own party the revolutionary impetus of February engendered at first an extreme confusion of political perspectives. As a matter of fact, during the July days, *Pravda* had a position much closer to revolutionary defensism than to the position of Lenin.

'When one army stands opposed to another army,' we read in one of its editorial articles, 'no policy could be more absurd than the policy of proposing that one of them should lay down arms and go home. Such a policy would not be a policy of peace, but a policy of enslavement, a policy to be scornfully rejected by a free people. No. The people will remain intrepidly at their post, answering bullet with bullet and shell with shell. This is beyond dispute. We must not allow any disorganization of the armed forces of the revolution.'[4] We find here no mention of classes, of the oppressors and the oppressed; there is, instead, talk of a 'free people'; there are no classes struggling for power but, instead, a free people are 'remaining at their post'. The ideas as well as the formulas are defensist through and through! And further in the same article: 'Our slogan is not the empty cry "Down with war!" which means the disorganization of the revolutionary army and of the army that is becoming ever more revolutionary. Our slogan is to bring pressure [!] to bear on the Provisional Government so as to compel it to make, without fail, openly and before the eyes of world democracy [!], an attempt [!] to induce [!] all the warring countries to initiate immediate negotiations to end the world war. Till then let everyone [!] remain at his post [!].'

The program of exerting pressure on an imperialist government so as to 'induce' it to pursue a pious course was the program of Kautsky and Ledebour in Germany, Jean Longuet in France, MacDonald in England; but it was never the program of Bolshevism. In conclusion, the article not only extends the 'warmest greetings' to the notorious manifesto of the Petrograd Soviet addressed 'To the Peoples of the World' (a manifesto permeated from beginning to end with the spirit of revolutionary defensism), but underscores 'with pleasure' the solidarity of the editorial board with the openly defensist resolutions adopted at two meetings in Petrograd. Of these resolutions it is enough to say that one runs as follows: 'If the democratic forces in Germany and Austria pay no heed to our voice [i.e. the 'voice' of the Provisional Government and of the conciliationist *soviet*]*, then we shall defend our fatherland to the last drop of our blood.'[5]

The above-quoted article is not an exception. On the contrary it quite accurately expresses the position of *Pravda*— prior to Lenin's return to Russia. Thus, in the next issue of the paper, in an article 'On the War', although it contains some criticism of the 'Manifesto of the Peoples of the World', the following occurs: 'It is impossible not to hail yesterday's proclamation of the Petrograd Soviet of Workers' and Soldiers' Deputies to the peoples of the world, summoning them to force their governments to bring the slaughter to an end.'[6] And where should a way out of the war be sought? The article gives the following answer: 'The way out is the path of bringing pressure to bear on the Provisional Government with the demand that the government proclaim its readiness to begin immediate negotiations for peace.'

We could adduce many similar quotations, covertly defensist and conciliationist in character. During the same period, and even weeks earlier, Lenin, who had not yet freed himself from his Zurich cage, was thundering in his 'Letters from Afar' (most of these letters never reached *Pravda*) against the faintest hint of any concessions to defensism and conciliationism. 'It is absolutely impermissible,' he wrote on

---

*   This is Trotsky's own addition.

9 March, discerning the image of revolutionary events in the distorted mirror of capitalist dispatches, 'it is absolutely impermissible to conceal from ourselves and from the people that this government wants to continue the imperialist war, that it is an agent of British capital, that it wants to restore the monarchy and strengthen the rule of the landlords and capitalists.' And later, on 12 March, he said: 'To urge that government to conclude a democratic peace is like preaching virtue to brothel keepers.' At the time when *Pravda* was advocating 'exerting pressure' on the Provisional Government in order to induce it to intervene in favor of peace 'before the eyes of world democracy', Lenin was writing: 'To urge the Guchkov-Milyukov government to conclude a speedy, honest, democratic and good-neighbourly peace is like the good village priest urging the landlords and the merchants to "walk in the way of God", to love their neighbours and to turn the other cheek.'[7]

On 4 April, the day after his arrival at Petrograd, Lenin came out decisively against the position of *Pravda* on the question of war and peace. He wrote: 'No support for the Provisional Government; the utter falsity of all its promises should be made clear, particularly of those relating to the renunciation of annexations. Exposure in place of the impermissible, illusion-breeding "demand" that *this* government, a government of capitalists, should *cease* to be an imperialist government.'[8] It goes without saying that the proclamation issued by the conciliators on 14 March, which had met with so many compliments from *Pravda*, was characterized by Lenin only as 'notorious' and 'muddled'. It is the height of hypocrisy to summon other nations to break with their

bankers while simultaneously forming a coalition government with the bankers of one's own country. "'The Centre" all
vow and declare that they are Marxists and internationalists,
that they are for peace, for bringing every kind of "pressure"
to bear upon the governments, for "demanding" in every way
that their own government should "ascertain the will of the
people for peace"."[9]

But here someone may at first glance raise an objection:
Ought a revolutionary party to refuse to 'exercise pressure'
on the bourgeoisie and its government? Certainly not. The
exercise of pressure on a bourgeois government is the road
of reform. A revolutionary Marxist party does not reject
reforms. But the road of reform serves a useful purpose in
subsidiary and not in fundamental questions. State power
cannot be obtained by reforms. 'Pressure' can never induce
the bourgeoisie to change its policy on a question that
involves its whole fate. The war created a revolutionary situation precisely by reason of the fact that it left no room for
any reformist 'pressure'. The only alternative was either to go
the whole way with the bourgeoisie, or to rouse the masses
against it so as to wrest the power from its hands. In the first
case it might have been possible to secure from the bourgeoisie some kind of sop with regard to home policy, on the
condition of unqualified support of their foreign imperialist policy. For this very reason social reformism transformed
itself openly, at the outset of the war, into social imperialism.
For the same reason the genuinely revolutionary elements
were forced to initiate the creation of this new International.

The point of view of *Pravda* was not proletarian and revolutionary but democratic-defensist, even though vacillating

in its defensism. We had overthrown tsarism, we should now exercise pressure on our own democratic government. The latter must propose peace to the peoples of the world. If the German democracy proves incapable of exerting due pressure on its own government, then we shall defend our 'fatherland' to the last drop of blood. The prospect of peace is not posed as an independent task of the working class which the workers are called upon to achieve over the head of the Provisional Government, because the conquest of power by the proletariat is not posed as a practical revolutionary task. Yet these two tasks are inextricably bound together.

Chapter Four
The April Conference

THE SPEECH which Lenin delivered at the Finland railway station on the socialist character of the Russian revolution was a bombshell to many leaders of the party. The polemic between Lenin and the partisans of 'completing the democratic revolution' began from the very first day.

A sharp conflict took place over the armed April demonstration, which raised the slogan: 'Down with the Provisional Government!' This incident supplied some representatives of the right wing with a pretext for accusing Lenin of Blanquism.* The overthrow of the Provisional Government, which was supported at that time by the *soviet* majority, could be accomplished, if you please, only by disregarding the majority of the toilers.

From a formal standpoint, such an accusation might seem rather plausible, but in point of fact there was not the slightest shade of Blanquism in Lenin's April policy. For Lenin

---

* Louis-Auguste Blanqui (1805–81) and his followers argued in favour of armed insurrection by small groups of conspirators, as opposed to the Marxist concept of mass revolutionary action.

the whole question hinged on the extent to which the *soviets* continued to reflect the real mood of the masses, and whether or not the party was mistaken in guiding itself by the *soviet* majority. The April demonstration, which went further 'to the left' than was warranted, was a kind of reconnoitering sortie to test the temper of the masses and the reciprocal relationship between them and the *soviet* majority. This reconnoitering operation led to the conclusion that a lengthy preparatory period was necessary. And we observe that Lenin in the beginning of May, sharply curbed the men from Kronstadt, who had gone too far and had declared against the recognition of the Provisional Government . . .

The opponents of the struggle for power had an entirely different approach to this question. At the April Party Conference, Comrade Kamenev made the following complaint: 'In No. 19 of *Pravda*, a resolution was first proposed by comrades [the reference here is obviously to Lenin]* to the effect that we should overthrow the Provisional Government. It appeared in print prior to the last crisis, and this slogan was later rejected as tending to disorganization; and it was recognized as adventuristic. This implies that our comrades learned something during this crisis. The resolution which is now proposed [by Lenin]* repeats that mistake . . . '

This manner of formulating the question is most highly significant. Lenin, after the experience of the reconnoiter, withdrew the slogan of the immediate overthrow of the Provisional Government. But he did not withdraw it for any set period of time—for so many weeks or months—but

* Both additions are Trotsky's.

stricly in dependence upon how quickly the revolt of the masses against the conciliationists would grow. The opposition, on the contrary, considered the slogan itself to be a blunder. In the temporary retreat of Lenin there was not even a hint of a change in the political line. He did not proceed from the fact that the democratic revolution was still uncompleted. He based himself exclusively on the idea that the masses were not at the moment capable of overthrowing the Provisional Government and that, therefore, everything possible had to be done to enable the working class to overthrow the Provisional Government on the morrow.

The whole of the April Party Conference was devoted to the following fundamental question: Are we heading toward the conquest of power in the name of the socialist revolution or are we helping (anybody and everybody) to complete the democratic revolution? Unfortunately, the report of the April Conference remains unpublished to this very day, though there is scarcely another congress in the history of our party that had such an exceptional and immediate bearing on the destiny of our revolution as the conference of April 1917.

Lenin's position was this: an irreconcilable struggle against defensism and its supporters; the capture of the *soviet* majority; the overthrow of the Provisional Government; the seizure of power through the *soviets*; a revolutionary peace policy and a program of socialist revolution at home and of international revolution abroad. In distinction to this, as we already know, the opposition held the view that it was necessary to complete the democratic revolution by exerting pressure on the Provisional Government, and in this process the *soviets* would remain the organs of 'control' over the power of the bourgeoisie. Hence flows quite another and incomparably more conciliatory attitude to defensism.

One of the opponents of Lenin's position argued in the following manner at the April Conference: 'We speak of the *soviets* of workers' and soldiers' deputies as if they were the organizing centers of our own forces and of state power . . . Their very name shows that they constitute a bloc of petty-bourgeois and proletarian forces which are still confronted with uncompleted bourgeois democratic tasks. Had the bourgeois democratic revolution been completed, this bloc would no longer exist . . . and the proletariat would be waging a revolutionary struggle against the bloc . . . And, nevertheless, we recognize these *soviets* as centers for the organization of forces . . . Consequently, the bourgeois revolution is not yet completed, it has not yet outlived itself; and I believe that all of us ought to recognize that with the complete accomplishment of this revolution, the power would actually have passed into the hands of the proletariat' (from the speech of Comrade Kamenev).

The hopeless schematism of this argument is obvious enough. For the crux of the matter lies precisely in the fact that the 'complete accomplishment of this revolution' could never take place without changing the bearers of power. The above speech ignores the class axis of the revolution; it deduces the task of the party not from the actual grouping of class forces but from a formal definition of the revolution as bourgeois, or as bourgeois-democratic. We are to participate in a bloc with the petty bourgeoisie and exercise control over the bourgeois power until the bourgeois revolution has been completely accomplished. The pattern is obviously

Menshevik. Limiting in a doctrinaire fashion the tasks of the revolution by its nomenclature (a 'bourgeois' revolution), one could not fail to arrive at the policy of exercising control over the Provisional Government and demanding that the Provisional Government should bring forward a policy of peace without annexations, and so on. By the completion of the democratic revolution was understood a series of reforms to be effected through the Constituent Assembly! Moreover, the Bolshevik Party was assigned the role of a left wing in the Constituent Assembly.

Such an outlook deprived the slogan 'All power to the *soviets!*' of any actual meaning. This was best and most consistently and most thoroughly expressed at the April Conference by the late Nogin, who also belonged to the opposition: 'In the process of development the most important functions of the *soviets* will fall away. A whole series of administrative functions will be transferred to the municipal, district, and other institutions. If we examine the future development of the structure of the state, we cannot deny that the Constituent Assembly will be convoked and after that the Parliament . . . Thus, it follows that the most important functions of the *soviets* will gradually wither away. That, however, does not mean to say that the *soviets* will end their existence in ignominy. They will only transfer their functions. Under these same *soviets* we shall not achieve the commune-republic in our country.'

Finally, a third opponent dealt with the question from the standpoint that Russia was not ready for socialism. 'Can we count on the support of the masses if we raise the slogan of proletarian revolution? Russia is the most petty-bourgeois country in Europe. To count on the sympathy of the masses for a socialist revolution is impossible; and, consequently, the more the party holds to the standpoint of a socialist revolution the further it will be reduced to the role of a propaganda circle. The impetus to a socialist revolution must come from the West.' And further on: 'Where will the sun of the socialist revolution rise? I believe that, in view of all the circumstances and our general cultural level, it is not for us to initiate the socialist revolution. We lack the necessary forces; the objective conditions for it do not exist in our country. But for the West this question is posed much in the same manner as the question of overthrowing tsarism in our country.'

Not all the opponents of Lenin's point of view at the April Conference drew the same conclusions as Nogin— but all of them were logically forced to accept these conclusions several months later, on the eve of October. Either we must assume leadership of the proletarian revolution or we must accept the role of an opposition in a bourgeois parliament—that is how the question was posed within our party. It is perfectly obvious that the latter position was essentially a Menshevik position, or rather the position which the Mensheviks found themselves compelled to occupy after the February revolution. As a matter of fact, the Mensheviks had for many years tapped away like so many woodpeckers at the idea that the coming revolution could only perform bourgeois tasks; that the social democracy could not take upon itself the tasks of bourgeois democracy and must remain an opposition while 'pushing the bourgeoisie to the left'. This theme was developed with a particularly boring profundity by Martynov. With the inception of the bourgeois revolution in 1917, the Mensheviks soon found themselves on the staff of the government. Out of their entire 'principled' position there remained only one political conclusion, namely, that the proletariat dare not seize power. But it is plain enough that those Bolsheviks who indicted Menshevik ministerialism and who at the same time were opposed to the seizure of power by the proletariat were, in point of fact, shifting to the pre-revolutionary positions of the Mensheviks.

The revolution caused political shifts to take place in two directions: the reactionaries became Cadets* and the Cadets became republicans against their own wishes—a purely formal shift to the left; the Social Revolutionaries and the Mensheviks became the ruling bourgeois party—a shift to the right. These are the means whereby bourgeois society seeks to create for itself a new backbone for state power, stability, and order. But at the time time, while the Mensheviks were passing from a formal socialist position to a vulgar democratic one, the right wing of the Bolsheviks was shifting to a formal socialist position, i.e. the Menshevik position of yesterday.

The same regroupment of forces took place on the question of war. The bourgeoisie, except for a few doctrinaires, kept wearily droning the same tune: no annexations, no indemnities—all the more so because the hopes for annexation were already very slim. The Zimmerwaldian Mensheviks** and

---

*   These were the Constitutional Democrats, who wanted to see a constitutional monarchy in Russia.
** This is a reference to the Zimmerwald conference of September 1915, at which various socialist groups declared their opposition to the war, including a section of the Russian Menshevik Party, which was split on the issue.

the SRs, who had criticized the French socialists because they defended their bourgeois republican fatherland, themselves immediately became defensists the moment they felt themselves part of a bourgeois republic. From a passive internationalist position, they shifted to an active patriotic one. At the same time, the right wing of the Bolsheviks went over to a passive internationalist position (exerting 'pressure' on the Provisional Government for the sake of a democratic peace, 'without annexations and without indemnities').

Thus at the April Conference the formula of the democratic dictatorship of the proletariat and the peasantry was driven asunder both theoretically and politically, and from it emerged two antagonistic points of view: a democratic point of view, camouflaged by formal socialist reservations, and a revolutionary socialist point of view, the genuinely Bolshevik and Leninist point of view.

Chapter Five
The July Days, the Kornilov episode, the Democratic Conference and the Pre-parliament

THE DECISIONS of the April Conference gave the party a correct principled orientation but they did not liquidate the disagreements among the party leaders. On the contrary, with the march of events, these disagreements assume more concrete forms, and reach their sharpest expression during the most decisive moment of the revolution—in the October days.

The attempt to organize a demonstration on 10 June (on Lenin's initiative) was denounced as an adventure by the very same comrades who had been dissatisfied with the character of the April demonstration. The demonstration of 10 June did not take place because it was proscribed by the Congress of Soviets. But on 18 June the party avenged itself. The general demonstration at Petrograd, which the conciliators had rather imprudently initiated, took place almost wholly under

Bolshevik slogans. Nevertheless, the government sought to have its own way. It light-mindedly ordered the idiotic offensive at the front. The moment was decisive. Lenin kept warning the party against imprudent steps. On 21 June, he wrote in *Pravda*: 'Comrades, a demonstrative act at this juncture would be inexpedient. We are now compelled to live through an entirely new stage in our revolution.' But the July days impended—an important landmark on the road of revolution, as well as on the road of the internal party disagreements.

In the July movement, the decisive moment came with the spontaneous onslaught by the Petrograd masses. It is indubitable that in July Lenin was weighing in his mind questions like these: Has the time come? Has the mood of the masses outgrown the *soviet* superstructure? Are we running the risk of becoming hypnotized by *soviet* legality, and of lagging behind the mood of the masses, and of being severed from them? It is very probable that isolated and purely military operations during the July days were initiated by comrades who honestly believed that they were not diverging from Lenin's estimate of the situation. Lenin afterwards said: 'We did a great many foolish things in July.' But the gist of the July days was that we made another, a new and much more extensive reconnoiter on a new and higher stage of the movement. We had to make a retreat, under onerous conditions. The party, to the extent that it was preparing for the insurrection and the seizure of power, considered—as did Lenin—that the July demonstration was only an episode in which we had to pay dearly for an exploration of our own strength and the enemy's, but which could not alter the main line of our activity.

On the other hand, the comrades who were opposed to the policy aimed at the seizure of power were bound to see a pernicious adventure in the July episode. The mobilization of the right-wing elements in the party became increasingly intensive; their criticism became more outspoken. There was also a corresponding change in the tone of rebuttal. Lenin wrote: 'All this whining, all these arguments to the effect that we "should not have" participated (in the attempt to lend a "peaceable and organized" character to the perfectly legitimate popular discontent and indignation!!), are either sheer apostasy, if coming from Bolsheviks, or the usual expression of the usual cowed and confused state of the petty bourgeoisie.'[10] The use of the word 'apostasy' at such a time sheds a tragic light upon the disagreements. As the events unfolded, this ominous word appeared more and more ofen.

The opportunist attitude toward the question of power and the question of war determined, of course, a corresponding attitude toward the International. The rights made an attempt to draw the party into the Stockholm Conference* of the social patriots. Lenin wrote on 16 August: 'The speech made by Comrade Kamenev on 6 August in the Central Executive Committee on the Stockholm Conference cannot but meet

---

* The Scandinavian socialist parties called an international peace conference in summer 1917 and invited the executive committee of the *soviets*. The Mensheviks and SRs accepted. Of the Bolsheviks, Kamenev supported the idea but Lenin argued that the conference was a political manoeuvre by the German government, working through those German socialists who were part of the wartime coalition, to feel out advantageous peace terms. The Bolsheviks' April Conference rejected the invitation.

with reproof from all Bolsheviks who are faithful to their Party and principles.' And further on, in reference to certain statements alleging that a great revolutionary banner was being unfurled over Stockholm, Lenin said: 'This is a meaningless declamation in the spirit of Chernov and Tseretelli.* It is a blatant untruth. In actual fact, it is not the revolutionary banner that is beginning to wave over Stockholm, but the banner of deals, agreements, amnesty for the social imperialists, and negotiations among bankers for dividing up annexed territory.'[11]

The road to Stockholm was, in effect, the road to the Second International, just as taking part in the Pre-Parliament was the road to the bourgeois republic. Lenin was *for* the boycott of the Stockholm Conference, just as later he was *for* the boycott of the Pre-Parliament. In the very heat of the struggle he did not for a single moment forget the tasks of creating a new Communist International.

As early as 10 April, Lenin came forward with a proposal to change the name of the party. All objections against the new name he characterized as follows: 'It is an argument of routinism, an argument of inertia, an argument of stagnation . . . It is time to cast off the soiled shirt and to put on clean linen.'[12] Nevertheless, the opposition of the party leaders was so strong that a whole year had to pass by—in the course of which all of Russia cast off the filthy garments of bourgeois domination—before the party could make up its mind to take a new name, returning to the tradition of Marx and Engels. This incident of renaming the party serves as a

---

* Chernov and Tseretelli were ministers in the Provisional Government.

symbolic expression of Lenin's role throughout the whole of 1917: during the sharpest turning point in history, he was all the while waging an intense struggle within the party against the day that had passed in the name of the day to come. And the opposition, belonging to the day that had passed, marching under the banner of 'tradition', became at times aggravated to the extreme.

The Kornilov events,* which created an abrupt shift in the situation in our favor, acted to soften the differences temporarily; they were softened but not eliminated. In the right wing, a tendency manifested itself during those days to draw closer to the *soviet* majority on the basis of defending the revolution and, in part, the fatherland. Lenin's reaction to this was expressed in his letter to the Central Committee at the beginning of September: 'It is my conviction that those who become unprincipled are people who . . . ** slide into defensism or (like other Bolsheviks) into a *bloc* with the SRs, into *supporting* the Provisional Government. Their attitude is absolutely wrong and unprincipled. We shall become defensists *only after* the transfer of power to the proletariat . . . Even now we must not support Kerensky's government. This is unprincipled. We may be asked: aren't we going to fight against Kornilov? Of course we must! But this is not the same

---

* General Kornilov, appointed commander-in-chief by the Provisional Government, attempted a coup in September 1917. See Cliff, *Lenin: All power to the Soviets*, pages 294–314.

** Trotsky's own note adds: 'From the construction of the latter part of the sentence, it is clear that a reference to certain names has been omitted here.' The 1966 edition of Lenin's Collected Works reads: '(like Volodarsky)'.

thing; there is a dividing line here, which is being stepped over by some Bolsheviks who fall into compromise and allow themselves to be *carried away* by the course of events.'[13]

The next stage in the evolution of divergent views was the Democratic Conference (14–22 September) and the Pre-Parliament that followed it (7 October).* The task of the Mensheviks and the SRs consisted in entangling the Bolsheviks in *soviet* legality and afterwards painlessly transforming the latter into bourgeois parliamentary legality. The rights were ready to welcome this. We are already acquainted with their manner of portraying the future development of the revolution: the *soviets* would gradually surrender their functions to corresponding institutions—to the *Dumas*, the *Zemstvos*, the trade unions, and finally to the Constituent Assembly—and would automatically vanish from the scene. Through the channel of the Pre-Parliament, the political awareness of the masses was to be directed away from the *soviets* as 'temporary' and dying institutions, to the Constituent Assembly as the crowning work of the democratic revolution. Meanwhile, the Bolsheviks were already in the majority in the Petrograd and Moscow *soviets*; our influence in the army grew, not from day to day, but from hour to hour. It was no longer a question of prognosis or perspective; it was literally a question of how we were to act the next day.

The conduct of the completely drained conciliationist parties at the Democratic Conference was the incarnation

---

* Both the Democratic Conference and the Pre-Parliament were attempts by the Mensheviks to set up an alternative to the *soviets*, where their support was fading.

of petty vileness. Yet the proposal which we introduced to abandon the Democratic Conference demonstratively, leaving it to its doom, met with decisive opposition on the part of the right elements of the fraction who were still influential at the top. The clash on this question was a prelude to the struggle over the question of boycotting the Pre-Parliament. On 24 September, i.e. after the Democratic Conference, Lenin wrote: 'The Bolsheviks should have walked out of the meeting in protest and not allowed themselves to be caught by the conference trap set to divert the people's attention from serious questions.'[14]

The discussion in the Bolshevik fraction at the Democratic Conference over the question of boycotting the Pre-Parliament had an exceptional importance despite the comparatively narrow scope of the issue itself. As a matter of fact, it was the most extensive and, on the surface, most successful attempt on the part of the rights to turn the party onto the path of 'completing the democratic revolution'. Apparently no minutes of these discussions were taken; in any case, no record has remained; to my knowledge even the secretary's notes have not been located as yet. The editors of this volume found a few scanty documents among my own papers. Comrade Kamenev expounded a line of argument which, later on, was developed in a sharper and more defined form and embodied in the well-known letter of Kamenev and Zinoviev (dated 11 October) to the party organizations. The most principled formulation of the question was made by Nogin: the boycott of the Pre-Parliament is a summons to an insurrection, i.e. to a repetition of the July days. Other comrades based themselves on general considerations of social democratic parliamentary tactics. No one would dare—so they said in substance—to propose that we boycott the Parliament; nevertheless, a proposal is made that we boycott an identical institution merely because it is called a *Pre-Parliament*.

The basic conception of the rights was as follows: the revolution must inevitably lead from the *soviets* to the establishment of bourgeois parliamentarism; the 'Pre-Parliament' forms a natural link in this process; therefore, it is folly to refuse to take part in the Pre-Parliament in view of our readiness to occupy the left benches in the Parliament itself. It was necessary to complete the democratic revolution and 'prepare' for the socialist revolution. How were we to prepare? By passing through the school of bourgeois parliamentarism; because, you see, the advanced country shows the backward country the image of its own future. The downfall of the tsarist monarchy is viewed as revolutionary—and so it was—but the conquest of power by the proletariat is conceived in a parliamentary way, on the basis of a completely accomplished democracy. Many long years of a democratic regime must elapse in the interval between the bourgeois revolution and the proletarian revolution. The struggle for our participation in the Pre-Parliament was the struggle for the 'Europeanization' of the working-class movement, for directing it as quickly as possible into the channel of a democratic 'struggle for power', i.e. into the channel of social democracy. Our fraction in the Democratic Conference, numbering over a hundred individuals, did not differ greatly, especially during those days, from a party congress. The majority of the fraction expressed itself in favor of participating in the Pre-Parliament. This fact was itself sufficient cause for alarm; and from that moment Lenin did sound the alarm unceasingly.

While the Democratic Conference was in session, Lenin wrote: 'It would be a big mistake, sheer parliamentary cretinism on our part, if we were to regard the Democratic Conference as a parliament; for even *if it were* to proclaim itself a permanent and sovereign parliament of the revolution, it would nevertheless *decide nothing*. The power of decision lies *outside it* in the working-class quarters of Petrograd and Moscow.'[15] Lenin's appraisal of the importance of participation or non-participation in the Pre-Parliament can be gathered from many of his declarations and particularly from his letter of 29 September to the Central Committee, in which he speaks of 'such glaring errors on the part of the Bolsheviks as the shameful decision to participate in the Pre-Parliament.'[16] For him this decision was an expression of the same democratic illusions and petty-bourgeois vacillations against which he had fought, developing and perfecting in the course of that struggle his conception of the proletarian revolution.

It is not true that many years must elapse between the bourgeois and proletarian revolutions. It is not true that the school of parliamentarism is the one and only, or the main, or the compulsory training school for the conquest of power. It is not true that the road to power runs necessarily through bourgeois democracy. These are all naked abstractions, doctrinaire patterns, and they play only one political role, namely, to bind the proletarian vanguard hand and foot, and by means of the 'democratic' state machinery turn it into an oppositionist political shadow of the bourgeoisie, bearing the name of social democracy. The policy of the proletariat must not be guided by schoolboy patterns but in accordance with the real flux of the class struggle. Our task is not to go to the Pre-Parliament but to organize the insurrection and seize power. The rest will follow. Lenin even proposed to call an emergency party congress, advancing as a platform the boycott of the Pre-Parliament. Henceforth all his letters and articles hammer at a single point: we must go, not into the Pre-Parliament to act as a 'revolutionary' tail of the conciliators, but out into the streets—to struggle for power!

Chapter Six
On the eve of the October revolution, the aftermath

AN EMERGENCY CONGRESS proved unnecessary. The pressure exerted by Lenin secured the requisite shift of forces to the left, both within the Central Committee and in our fraction in the Pre-Parliament. The Bolsheviks withdrew from it on 10 October. In Petrograd the *soviet* clashed with the government over the order transferring to the front the part of the garrison which sympathized with the Bolsheviks. On 16 October, the Revolutionary Military Committee was created, the legal *soviet* organ of insurrection. The right wing of the party sought to retard the development of events. The struggle of tendencies within the party, as well as the class struggle in the country, entered its decisive phase.

The position of the rights is best and most completely illumined in its principled aspects by a letter signed by Zinoviev and Kamenev and entitled 'On the Current Situation'. The letter was written on 11 October, that is, two weeks before the insurrection, and it was sent to the most important party organizations. The letter comes out in decisive opposition to the resolution for an armed insurrection adopted by the Central Committee. Cautioning against underestimating the enemy, while in reality monstrously underestimating the forces of revolution and even denying that the masses are in a mood for battle (two weeks before 25 October!), the letter states: 'We are deeply convinced that to call at present for an armed uprising means to stake on one card not only the fate of our party but also the fate of the Russian and international revolution.' But if the insurrection and the seizure of power are out of the question, what then? The answer in the letter is also quite plain and precise: 'Through the army, through the workers, we hold a revolver at the temple of the bourgeoisie,' and because of this revolver the bourgeoisie will be unable to quash the Constituent Assembly. 'The chances of our party in the elections to the Constituent Assembly are excellent . . . The influence of the Bolsheviks is increasing . . . With correct tactics we can get a third and even more of the seats in the Constituent Assembly.'

Thus, this letter openly steers a course towards our playing the role of an 'influential' opposition in a bourgeois Constituent Assembly. This purely social democratic course is superficially camouflaged by the following consideration: 'The *soviets*, which have become rooted in life, cannot be destroyed. The Constituent Assembly will be able to find support for its revolutionary work only in the *soviets*. The Constituent Assembly plus the *soviets*—that is that combined type of state institution towards which we are going.' It is of extraordinary interest with regard to characterizing the entire line of the rights that the theory of 'combined' state forms, the correlation of the Constituent Assembly with the *soviets*, was reiterated in Germany a year and a half or two years later by Rudolf Hilferding, who also waged a struggle against the seizure of power by the proletariat. The Austro-German opportunist was unaware that he was plagiarizing.

The letter 'On the Current Situation' refutes the assertion that the majority of the people in Russia were already supporting us, on the basis of a purely parliamentary estimate of this majority. 'In Russia a majority of the workers,' the letter states, 'and a substantial part of the soldiers are with us. But all the rest is dubious. We are all convinced, for instance, that if elections to the Constituent Assembly were to take place now, a majority of the peasants would vote for the SRs. What is this, an accident?'

The above formulation of the question contains the principal and fundamental error, flowing from a failure to understand that the peasants might have strong revolutionary interests and an intense urge to realize them, but cannot have an independent political position. They might either vote for the bourgeoisie, by voting for its SR agency, or join in action with the proletariat. Which one of these two possibilities would materialize hinged precisely upon the policy we pursued. Had we gone to the Pre-Parliament in order to constitute an influential opposition ('a third and even more of the seats') in the Constituent Assembly, then we would have almost automatically placed the peasantry in such a position as would have compelled it to seek the satisfaction of its interests through the Constituent Assembly; and, consequently, they would have looked not to the opposition but to the majority.

On the other hand, the seizure of power by the proletariat immediately created the revolutionary framework for the struggle of the peasantry against the landlords and the officials. To use the expressions so current among us on this question, this letter expresses simultaneously both an *underestimation* and an *overestimation* of the peasantry. It underestimates the revolutionary potential of the peasants (under a proletarian leadership) and it overestimates their political independence. This twofold error of overestimating and at the same time underestimating the peasantry flows, in its turn, from an underestimation of our own class and its party—that is, from a social democratic approach to the proletariat. And this is not at all surprising. All shades of opportunism are, in the last analysis, reducible to an incorrect evaluation of the revolutionary forces and potential of the proletariat.

Objecting to the seizure of power, the letter tries to scare the party with the prospect of a revolutionary war. 'The masses of the soldiers support us not because of the slogan of war, but because of the slogan of peace . . . If, having taken power at present by ourselves, we should come to the conclusion (in view of the whole world situation) that it is necessary to wage a revolutionary war, the masses of soldiers will rush away from us. The best part of the army youth will, of course, remain with us, but the masses of the soldiers will turn away.' This line of reasoning is most highly instructive. We have here the basic arguments in favor of signing the Brest-Litovsk peace;* in the present instance, however, they

---

* This peace treaty between Soviet Russia and Germany was signed on 3 March 1918.

are being directed against the seizure of power. It is plain enough that the position expressed in the letter 'On the Current Situation' later facilitated in the highest degree the acceptance of the Brest-Litovsk peace by those who supported the views expressed in the above letter. It remains for us to repeat here what we said in another place, namely, that the political genius of Lenin is characterized not by taking the temporary Brest-Litovsk capitulation as an isolated fact but only by considering Brest-Litovsk in combination with October. This must always be kept in mind.

The working class struggles and matures in the never-failing consciousness of the fact that the preponderance of forces lies on the side of the enemy. This preponderance manifests itself in daily life, at every step. The enemy possesses wealth and state power, all the means of exerting ideological pressure and all the instruments of repression. We become habituated to the idea that the preponderance of forces is on the enemy's side; and this habitual thought enters as an integral part into the entire life and activity of the revolutionary party during the preparatory epoch. The consequences entailed by this or that careless or premature act serve each time as most cruel reminders of the enemy's strength.

But a moment comes when this habit of regarding the enemy as stronger becomes the main obstacle on the road to victory. Today's weakness of the bourgeoisie seems to be cloaked by the shadow of its strength of yesterday. 'You underestimate the strength of the enemy!' This cry serves as the axis for the grouping of all elements opposed to the armed insurrection. 'But everyone who does not want merely to talk about uprising,' wrote the opponents of insurrection in our own country, two weeks before our victory, 'must carefully weigh its chances. And here we consider it our duty to say that at the present moment it would be most harmful to underestimate the forces of our opponent and overestimate our own forces. The forces of the opponent are greater than they appear. Petrograd is decisive, and in Petrograd the enemies of the proletarian party have accumulated substantial forces: 5,000 military cadets, *excellently* armed, *organized, anxious* (because of their class position) and able to fight; also the staff, shock troops, Cossacks, a substantial part of the garrison, and very considerable artillery, which has taken up a position in fan-like formation around Petrograd. Then our adversaries will undoubtedly attempt, with the aid of the All-Russian Central Executive Committee of the Soviets, to bring troops from the front'.

In a civil war, to the extent that it is not a question of merely counting battalions beforehand but of drawing a rough balance of their state of consciousness, such an estimate can, of course, never prove completely satisfactory or adequate. Even Lenin estimated that the enemy had strong forces in Petrograd; and he proposed that the insurrection begin in Moscow where, as he thought, it might be carried out almost without bloodshed. Such partial mistakes of forecast are absolutely unavoidable even under the most favorable circumstances and it is always more correct to make plans in accordance with the less favorable conditions. But of interest to us in the given case is the fact that the enemy forces were monstrously overestimated and that all proportions were completely distorted at a time when the enemy was actually deprived of any armed force.

This question—as the experience of Germany proved—is of paramount importance. So long as the slogan of insurrection was approached by the leaders of the German Communist Party mainly, if not solely, from an agitational standpoint, they simply ignored the question of the armed forces at the disposal of the enemy (Reichswehr, fascist detachments, police, etc.). It seemed to them that the constantly rising revolutionary flood tide would automatically solve the military question. But when the task stared them in the face, the very same comrades who had previously treated the armed forces of the enemy as if they were nonexistent, went immediately to the other extreme. They placed implicit faith in all the statistics of the armed strength of the bourgeoisie, meticulously added to the latter the forces of the Reichswehr and the police; then they reduced the whole to a round number (half a million and more) and so obtained a compact mass force armed to the teeth and absolutely sufficient to paralyze their own efforts.

No doubt the forces of the German counter-revolution were much stronger numerically and, at any rate, better organized and prepared than our own Kornilovites and semi-Kornilovites. But so were the effective forces of the German revolution. The proletariat composes the overwhelming majority of the population in Germany. In our country, the question—at least during the initial stage—was decided by Petrograd and Moscow. In Germany, the insurrection would have immediately blazed in scores of mighty proletarian centers. On this arena, the armed forces of the enemy would not have seemed nearly as terrible as they did in statistical computations, expressed in round figures. In any case, we must categorically reject the tendentious calculations which were made, and which are still being made, after the debacle of the German October, in order to justify the policy that led to the debacle.

Our Russian example is of great significance in this connection. Two weeks prior to our bloodless victory in Petrograd—and we could have gained it even two weeks earlier—experienced party politicians saw arrayed against us the military cadets, anxious and able to fight, the shock troops, the Cossacks, a substantial part of the garrison, the artillery, in fan-like formation, and the troops arriving from the front. But in reality all this came to nothing: in round figures, zero. Now, let us imagine for a moment that the opponents of the insurrection had carried the day in our party and in the Central Committee. The part that leadership plays in a civil war is all too clear: in such a case the revolution would have been doomed beforehand—unless Lenin had appealed to the party against the Central Committee, which he was preparing to do, and in which he would undoubtedly have been successful. But, under similar conditions, not every party will have its Lenin . . .

It is not difficult to imagine how history would have been written, had the line of evading the battle carried in the Central Committee. The official historians would, of course, have explained that an insurrection in October 1917 would have been sheer madness; and they would have furnished the reader with awe-inspiring statistical charts of the military cadets and Cossacks and shock troops and artillery, in fan-like formation, and army corps arriving from the front. Never tested in the fire of insurrection, these forces would have seemed immeasurably more terrible than they proved in action. Here is the lesson which must be burned into the consciousness of every revolutionist!

The persistent, tireless, and incessant pressure which Lenin exerted on the Central Committee throughout September and October arose from his constant fear lest we allow the propitious moment to slip away. All this is nonsense, replied the rights, our influence will continue to grow. Who was right? And what does it mean to lose the propitious moment? This question directly involves an issue on which the Bolshevik estimate of the ways and means of revolution comes into sharpest and clearest conflict with the social democratic, Menshevik estimate: the former being active, strategic, and practical through and through, while the latter is utterly permeated with fatalism.

What does it mean to lose the propitious moment? The most favorable conditions for an insurrection exist, obviously, when the maximum shift in our favor has occurred in the relationship of forces. We are, of course, referring to the relationship of forces in the domain of consciousness, i.e. in the domain of the political superstructure, and not in the domain of the economic foundation, which may be assumed to remain more or less unchanged throughout the entire revolutionary epoch. On one and the same economic foundation, with one and the same class division of society, the relationship of forces changes depending upon the mood of the proletarian masses, the extent to which their illusions are shattered and their political experience has grown, the extent to which the confidence of intermediate classes and groups in the state power is shattered, and finally the extent to which the latter loses confidence in itself.

During revolution all these processes take place with lightning speed. The whole tactical art consists in this: that we seize the moment when the combination of circumstances is most favorable to us. The Kornilov uprising completely prepared such a combination. The masses, having lost confidence in the parties of the *soviet* majority, saw with their own eyes the danger of counter-revolution. They came to the conclusion that it was now up to the Bolsheviks to find a way out of the situation. Neither the elemental disintegration of the state power nor the elemental influx of the impatient and exacting confidence of the masses in the Bolsheviks could endure for a protracted period of time. The crisis had to be resolved away one way or another. It is now or never! Lenin kept repeating.

The rights said in refutation: 'It would be a serious historical untruth to formulate the question of the transfer of power into the hands of the proletarian party in the terms: either now or never. No. The party of the proletariat will grow. Its program will become known to broader and broader masses . . . And there is only one way in which the proletarian party can interrupt its successes, and that is if under present conditions it takes upon itself to initiate an uprising . . . Against this perilous policy we raise our voice in warning.'

This fatalistic optimism deserves most careful study. There is nothing national and certainly nothing individual about it. Only last year we witnessed the very same tendency in Germany. This passive fatalism is really only a cover for irresolution and even incapacity for action, but it camouflages itself with the consoling prognosis that we are, you know, growing more and more influential; as time goes on, our forces will continually increase. What a gross delusion! The strength of a revolutionary party increases only up to a certain moment, after which the process can turn into the very opposite. The hopes of the masses change into disillusionment as a result of the party's passivity, while the enemy recovers from his panic and takes advantage of this disillusionment. We witnessed such a decisive turning point in Germany in October 1923. We were not so very far removed from a similar turn of events in Russia in the fall of 1917. For that, a delay of a few more weeks would perhaps have been enough. Lenin was right. It was *now* or *never*!

'But the decisive question'—and here the opponents of the insurrection brought forward their last and strongest argument—'is, is the sentiment among the workers and soldiers of the capital really such that they see salvation only in street fighting, that they are impatient to go into the streets? No. There is no such sentiment . . . If among the great masses of the poor of the capital there were a militant sentiment burning to go into the streets, it might have served as a guarantee that an uprising initiated by them would draw in the biggest organizations (railroad unions, unions of postal and telegraph workers, etc.), where the influence of our party is weak. But since there is no such sentiment even in the factories and barracks, it would be a self-deception to build any plans on it.'

These lines written on 11 October acquire an exceptional and most timely significance when we recall that the leading comrades in the German party, in their attempt to explain away their retreat last year without striking a blow, especially emphasized the reluctance of the masses to fight. But the very crux of the matter lies in the fact that a victorious insurrection becomes, generally speaking, most assured when the masses have had sufficient experience not to plunge headlong into the struggle but to wait and demand a resolute and capable fighting leadership. In October 1917, the working-class masses, or at least their leading section, had already come to the firm conviction—on the basis of the experience of the April demonstration, the July days, and the Kornilov events—that neither isolated elemental protests nor reconnoitering operations were any longer on the agenda—but a decisive insurrection for the seizure of power. The mood of the masses correspondingly became more concentrated, more critical, and more profound.

The transition from an illusory, exuberant, elemental mood to a more critical and conscious frame of mind necessarily implies a pause in revolutionary continuity. Such a progressive crisis in the mood of the masses can be overcome only by a proper party policy, that is to say, above all by the genuine readiness and ability of the party to lead the insurrection of the proletariat. On the other hand, a party which carries on a protracted revolutionary agitation, tearing the masses away from the influence of the conciliationists, and then, after the confidence of the masses has been raised to the utmost, begins to vacillate, to split hairs, to hedge, and to temporize—such a party paralyzes the activity of the masses, sows disillusion and disintegration among them, and brings ruin to the revolution; but in return it provides itself with the ready excuse—after the debacle—that the masses were insufficiently active. This was precisely the course steered by the letter 'On the Current Situation'. Luckily, our party under the leadership of Lenin was decisively able to liquidate such moods among the leaders. Because of this alone it was able to guide a victorious revolution.

We have characterized the nature of the political questions bound up with the preparation for the October Revolution, and we have attempted to clarify the gist of the differences that arose; and now it remains for us to trace briefly the most important moments of the internal party struggle during the last decisive weeks.

The resolution for an armed insurrection was adopted by the Central Committee on 10 October. On 11 October the letter 'On the Current Situation', analyzed above, was sent out to the most important party organizations. On 18 October, that is, a week before the revolution, *Novaya Zhizn* [New Life] published the letter of Kamenev. 'Not only Comrade Zinoviev and I,' we read in this letter, 'but also a number of practical comrades think that to assume the initiative of an armed insurrection at the present moment, with the given correlation of forces, independently of and several days before the Congress of Soviets, is an inadmissible step ruinous to the proletariat and to the revolution.'[17] On 25 October power was seized in Petrograd and the Soviet government was created.

On 4 November, a number of responsible party members resigned from the Central Committee of the party and from the Council of People's Commissars, and issued an ultimatum demanding the formation of a coalition government composed of all *soviet* parties. 'Otherwise,' they wrote, 'the only course that remains is to maintain a purely Bolshevik government by means of political terror."* And, in another document, issued at the same time: 'We cannot assume any responsibility for this ruinous policy of the Central Committee which has been adopted contrary to the will of the great majority of the proletariat and the soldiers who are longing for the quickest possible cessation of bloodshed between the different sections of democracy. For this reason we resign from our posts in the Central Committee in order to avail ourselves of the right to express our candid opinions to the masses of workers and soldiers and summon them to support our cry: "Long live the government of all *soviet* parties!" Immediate conciliation on this basis!'[18]

Thus, those who had opposed the armed insurrection and the seizure of power as an adventure were demanding, after the victorious conclusion of the insurrection, that the power be restored to those parties against whom the proletariat had to struggle in order to conquer power. And why, indeed, was the victorious Bolshevik Party obliged to restore power to the Mensheviks and the srs? (And it was precisely the restoration of power that was the question here!) To this the opposition replied: 'We consider that the creation of such a government is necessary for the sake of preventing further bloodshed, an imminent famine, the crushing of the revolution by Kaledin and his cohorts; and in order to insure the

---

*   The four Central Committee members who resigned were Kamenev, Zinoviev, Rykov and Nogin. Miliutin, Teodorovich, Rykov and Nogin resigned as People's Commissars. Within a matter of weeks, however, they had backed down and asked to be reinstated.

convocation of the Constituent Assembly and the actual carrying through of the program of peace adopted by the All-Russian Congress of Soviets of Soldiers' and Workers' Deputies.'[19] In other words, it was a question of clearing a path for bourgeois parliamentarianism through the portals of the *soviets*. The revolution had refused to pass through the Pre-Parliament, and had had to cut a channel for itself through October; therefore the task, as formulated by the opposition, consisted in saving the revolution from the dictatorship, with the help of the Mensheviks and the SRs, by diverting it into the channel of a bourgeois regime. What was in question here was the liquidation of October—no more, no less. Naturally, there could be no talk whatever of conciliation under such conditions.

On the next day, 5 November, still another letter, along the same lines, was published. 'I cannot, in the name of party discipline, remain silent when in the face of common sense and the elemental movement of the masses, Marxists refuse to take into consideration objective conditions which imperiously dictate to us, under the threat of a catastrophe, conciliation with all the socialist parties . . . I cannot, in the name of party discipline, submit to the cult of personal worship, and stake political conciliation with all socialist parties who agree to our basic demands, upon the inclusion of this or that individual in the ministry, nor am I willing for that reason to prolong the bloodshed even for a single minute.'[20] The author of this letter (Lozovsky) ends by declaring it urgent to fight for an emergency party congress which would decide the question 'whether the Russian Social Democratic Labor Party (Bolsheviks) will remain a Marxist working-class party or whether it will finally adopt a course which has nothing in common with revolutionary Marxism.'

The situation seemed perfectly hopeless. Not only the bourgeoisie and the landlords, not only the so-called 'revolutionary democracy' who still retained the control of the leading bodies of many organizations (the All-Russian Central Executive Committee of Railwaymen [*Vikzhel*], the army committees, the government employees, and so on) but also some of the most influential members of our own party, members of the Central Committee and the Council of People's Commissars, were loud in their public condemnation of the party's attempt to remain in power in order to carry out its program. The situation might have seemed hopeless, we repeat, if one looked only at the surface of events. What then remained? To acquiesce to the demands of the opposition meant to liquidate October. In that case, we should not have achieved it in the first place. Only one course was left: to march ahead, relying upon the revolutionary will of the masses.

On 7 November, *Pravda* carried the decisive declaration of the Central Committee of our party, written by Lenin, and permeated with real revolutionary fervor, expressed in clear, simple, and unmistakable formulations addressed to the rank and file of the party. This proclamation put an end to any doubt as to the future policy of the party and its Central Committee: 'Shame on all the faint-hearted, all the waverers and doubters, on all those who allowed themselves to be intimidated by the bourgeoisie or who have succumbed to the outcries of their direct and indirect supporters! *There is not the slightest* hesitation among the *mass* of the workers and soldiers of Petrograd, Moscow, and other places. Our party stands solidly and firmly, as one man, in defence of Soviet power, in defence of the interests of all the working people, and first and foremost of the workers and poor peasants.'[21]

The extremely acute party crisis was overcome. However, the internal party struggle did not yet cease. The main lines of the struggle still remained the same. But its political importance faded. We find most interesting evidence of this in a report made by Uritsky at a session of the Petrograd Committee of our party on 12 December, on the subject of convening the Constituent Assembly. 'The disagreements within our party are not new. We have here the same tendency which manifested itself previously on the question of the insurrection. Some comrades are now of the opinion that the Constituent Assembly is the crowning work of the revolution. They base their position on the book of etiquette. They say we must not act tactlessly, and so on. They object to the Bolsheviks, as members of the Constituent Assembly, deciding the date to convoke it, the relationship of forces in it, and so on. They look at things from a purely formal standpoint, leaving entirely out of consideration the fact that the exercise of this control is only a reflection of the events taking place outside the Constituent Assembly, and that with this consideration in mind we are able to outline our attitude toward the Constituent Assembly . . . At the present time our point of view is that we are fighting for the interests of the proletariat and the poor peasantry, while a handful of comrades consider that we are making a bourgeois revolution which must be crowned by the Constituent Assembly.'

The dissolution of the Constituent Assembly may be considered as marking the close not only of a great chapter in the history of Russia, but of an equally important chapter in the history of our party. By overcoming the internal friction, the party of the proletariat not only conquered power but was able to maintain it.

Chapter Seven
The October insurrection and *soviet* legality

IN SEPTEMBER, while the Democratic Conference was in session, Lenin demanded that we immediately proceed with the insurrection. 'In order to treat insurrection in a Marxist way, i.e. as an art, we must at the same time, without losing a single moment, organise a *headquarters* of the insurgent detachments, distribute our forces, move the reliable regiments to the most important points, surround the Alexandrinsky Theatre, occupy the Peter and Paul Fortress, arrest the General Staff and the government, and move against the officer cadets and the Savage Division those detachments which would rather die than allow the enemy to approach the strategic points of the city. We must mobilise the armed workers and call them to fight the last desperate fight, occupy the telegraph and telephone exchanges at once, move *our* insurrection headquarters to the central telephone exchange and connect it by telephone with all the factories, all the regiments, all the points of armed fighting, etc. Of course, this is all by way of example, only to *illustrate* the fact that at the present moment it is impossible to remain loyal to Marxism, to remain loyal to the revolution *unless insurrection is treated as an art.*'[22]

The above formulation of the question presupposed that the preparation and completion of the insurrection were to be carried out through party channels and in the name of the party, and afterwards the seal of approval was to be placed on the victory by the Congress of Soviets. The Central Committee did not adopt this proposal. The insurrection was led into *soviet* channels and was linked in our agitation with the Second Soviet Congress. A detailed explanation of this difference of opinion will make it clear that this question pertains not to principle but rather to a technical issue of great practical importance.

We have already pointed out with what intense anxiety Lenin regarded the postponement of the insurrection. In view of the vacillation among the party leaders, an agitation formally linking the impending insurrection with the impending Soviet Congress seemed to him an impermissible delay, a concession to the irresolute, a loss of time through vacillation, and an outright crime. Lenin kept reiterating this idea from the end of September onward.

'There is a tendency, or an opinion, in our Central Committee and among the leaders of our Party,' he wrote on 29 September, 'which favours *waiting* for the Congress of Soviets, and is *opposed* to taking power immediately, is *opposed* to an immediate insurrection. That tendency, or opinion, must be *overcome.*'[23]

At the beginning of October, Lenin wrote: 'Delay is criminal. To wait for the Congress of Soviets would be a childish game of formalities, a disgraceful game of formalities, and a betrayal of the revolution.'[24]

In his theses for the Petrograd Conference of 8 October, Lenin said: 'It is necessary to fight against constitutional illusions and hopes placed in the Congress of Soviets, to discard the preconceived idea that we absolutely must "wait" for it.'[25]

Finally, on 24 October, Lenin wrote: 'It is now absolutely clear that to delay the uprising would be fatal . . . History will not forgive revolutionaries for procrastinating when they could be victorious today (and they certainly will be victorious today), while they risk losing much tomorrow, in fact, they risk losing everything.'[26]

All these letters, every sentence of which was forged on the anvil of revolution, are of exceptional value in that they serve both to characterize Lenin and to provide an estimate of the situation at the time. The basic and all-pervasive thought expressed in them is—anger, protest, and indignation against a fatalistic, temporizing, social democratic, Menshevik attitude to revolution, as if the latter were an endless film. If time is, generally speaking, a prime factor in politics, then the importance of time increases a hundredfold in war and in revolution. It is not at all possible to accomplish on the morrow everything that can be done today. To rise in arms, to overwhelm the enemy, to seize power, may be possible today, but tomorrow may be impossible.

But to seize power is to change the course of history. Is it really true that such a historic event can hinge upon an interval of twenty-four hours? Yes, it can. When things have reached the point of armed insurrection, events are to be measured not by the long yardstick of politics, but by the short yardstick of war. To lose several weeks, several days, and sometimes even a single day, is tantamount under certain conditions to the surrender of the revolution, to capitulation. Had Lenin not sounded the alarm, had there not been all this pressure and criticism on his part, had it not been for his intense and passionate revolutionary mistrust, the party would probably have failed to align its front at the decisive moment, for the opposition among the party leaders was very strong, and the staff plays a major role in all wars, including civil wars.

At the same time, however, it is quite clear that to prepare the insurrection and to carry it out under cover of preparing for the Second Soviet Congress and under the slogan of defending it, was of inestimable advantage to us. From the moment when we, as the Petrograd Soviet, invalidated Kerensky's order transferring two-thirds of the garrison to the front, we had actually entered a state of armed insurrection. Lenin, who was not in Petrograd, could not appraise the full significance of this fact. So far as I remember, there is not a mention of it in all his letters during this period. Yet the outcome of the insurrection of 25 October was at least three-quarters settled, if not more, the moment that we opposed the transfer of the Petrograd garrison; created the Revolutionary Military Committee (16 October); appointed our own commissars in all army divisions and institutions; and thereby completely isolated not only the general staff of the Petrograd zone, but also the government. As a matter of fact, we had here an armed insurrection—an armed though bloodless insurrection of the Petrograd regiments against the Provisional Government—under the leadership of the

Revolutionary Military Committee and under the slogan of preparing the defense of the Second Soviet Congress, which would decide the ultimate fate of the state power.

Lenin's counsel to begin the insurrection in Moscow, where, on his assumptions, we could gain a bloodless victory, flowed precisely from the fact that in his underground refuge he had no opportunity to assess the radical turn that took place not only in mood but also in organizational ties among the military rank and file as well as the army hierarchy after the 'peaceful' insurrection of the garrison of the capital in the middle of October. The moment that the regiments, upon the instructions of the Revolutionary Military Committee, refused to depart from the city, we had a victorious insurrection in the capital, only slightly screened at the top by the remnants of the bourgeois democratic state forms. The insurrection of 25 October was only supplementary in character. This is precisely why it was painless. In Moscow, on the other hand, the struggle was much longer and bloodier, despite the fact that in Petrograd the power of the Council of People's Commissars had already been established. It is plain enough that had the insurrection begun in Moscow, prior to the overturn in Petrograd, it would have dragged on even longer, with the outcome very much in doubt. Failure in Moscow would have had grave effects on Petrograd. Of course, a victory along these lines was not at all excluded. But the way that events actually occurred proved much more economical, much more favorable, and much more successful.

We were more or less able to synchronize the seizure of power with the opening of the Second Soviet Congress only because the peaceful, almost 'legal' armed insurrection—at least in Petrograd—was already three-quarters, if not nine-tenths achieved. Our reference to this insurrection as 'legal' is in the sense that it was an outgrowth of the 'normal' conditions of dual power. Even when the conciliationists dominated the Petrograd Soviet it frequently happened that the *soviet* revised or amended the decisions of the government. This was, so to speak, part of the constitution of the regime that has been inscribed in the annals of history as the 'Kerensky period'. When we Bolsheviks assumed power in the Petrograd Soviet, we only continued and deepened the methods of dual power. We took it upon ourselves to revise the order transferring the troops to the front. By this very act we covered up the actual insurrection of the Petrograd garrison with the traditions and methods of legal dual power. Nor was that all. While formally adapting our agitation on the question of power to the opening of the Second Soviet Congress, we developed and deepened the already existing traditions of dual power, and prepared the framework of *soviet* legality for the Bolshevik insurrection on an All-Russian scale.

We did not lull the masses with any *soviet* constitutional illusions, for under the slogan of a struggle for the Second Soviet Congress we won over to our side the bayonets of the revolutionary army and consolidated our gains organizationally. And, in addition, we succeeded, far more than we expected, in luring our enemies, the conciliationists, into the trap of *soviet* legality. Resorting to trickery in politics, all the more so in revolution, is always dangerous. You will most likely fail to dupe the enemy, but the masses who follow you may be duped instead. Our 'trickery' proved

100 per cent successful—not because it was an artful scheme devised by wily strategists seeking to avoid a civil war, but because it derived naturally from the disintegration of the conciliationist regime with its glaring contradictions. The Provisional Government wanted to get rid of the garrison. The soldiers did not want to go to the front. We invested this natural unwillingness with a political expression; we gave it a revolutionary goal and a 'legal' cover. Thereby we secured unprecedented unanimity within the garrison, and bound it up closely with the Petrograd workers. Our opponents, on the contrary, because of their hopeless position and their muddleheadedness, were inclined to accept the *soviet* cover at its face value. They yearned to be deceived and we provided them with ample opportunity to gratify their desire.

Between the conciliationists and ourselves, there was a struggle for *soviet* legality. In the minds of the masses, the *soviets* were the source of all power. Out of the *soviets* came Kerensky, Tseretelli, and Skobelev. But we ourselves were closely bound up with the *soviets* through our basic slogan, *'All power to the soviets!'* The bourgeoisie derived their succession to power from the state Duma. The conciliationists derived their succession from the *soviets*; and so did we. But the conciliationists sought to reduce the *soviets* to nothing; while we were striving to transfer power to the *soviets*. The conciliationists could not break as yet with the *soviet* heritage, and were in haste to create a bridge from the latter to parliamentarism. With this in mind they convened the Democratic Conference and created the Pre-Parliament. The participation of the *soviets* in the Pre-Parliament gave a semblance of sanction to this procedure. The conciliationists sought to catch the revolution with the bait of *soviet* legality and, after hooking it, to drag it into the channel of bourgeois parliamentarism.

But we were also interested in making use of *soviet* legality. At the conclusion of the Democratic Conference we extracted from the conciliationists a promise to convene the Second Soviet Congress. This congress placed them in an extremely embarrassing position. On the one hand, they could not oppose convening it without breaking with *soviet* legality; on the other hand, they could not help seeing that the congress—because of its composition—boded them little good. In consequence, all the more insistently did we appeal to the Second Congress as the real master of the country; and all the more did we adapt our entire preparatory work to the support and defense of the Congress of Soviets against the inevitable attacks of the counter-revolution. If the conciliationists attempted to hook us with *soviet* legality through the Pre-Parliament emanating from the *soviets*, then we, on our part, lured them with the same *soviet* legality—through the Second Congress.

It is one thing to prepare an armed insurrection under the naked slogan of the seizure of power by the party, and quite another thing to prepare and then carry out an insurrection under the slogan of defending the rights of the Congress of Soviets. Thus, the adaptation of the question of the seizure of power to the Second Soviet Congress did not involve any naive hopes that the congress itself could settle the question of power. Such fetishism of the *soviet* form was entirely alien to us. All the necessary work for the conquest of power, not only the political but also the organizational and military-technical work for the seizure of power, went on at full speed. But the legal cover for all this work was always provided by an invariable reference to the coming congress, which would settle the question of power. Waging an offensive all along the line, we kept up the appearance of being on the defensive.

On the other hand, the Provisional Government—if it had been able to make up its mind to defend itself seriously—would have had to attack the Congress of Soviets, prohibit its convocation, and thereby provide the opposing side with a motive—most damaging to the government—for an armed insurrection. Moreover, we not only placed the Provisional Government in an unfavourable political position; we also lulled their already sufficiently lazy and unwieldy minds. These people seriously believed that we were only concerned with *soviet* parliamentarism, and with a new congress which would adopt a new resolution on power—in the style of the resolutions adopted by the Petrograd and Moscow *soviets*—and that the government would then ignore it, using the Pre-Parliament and the coming Constituent Assembly as a pretext, and thus put us in a ridiculous position.

We have the irrefutable testimony of Kerensky to the effect that the minds of the sagest middle-class wisea-cres were bent precisely in this direction. In his memoirs, Kerensky relates how, in his study, at midnight on 25 October, stormy disputes raged between himself, Dan, and the others over the armed insurrection, which was then in full swing. Kerensky says, 'Dan declared, first of all, that they were better informed than I was, and that I was exaggerating the events, under the influence of reports from my "reactionary staff".

He then informed me that the resolution adopted by the majority of the *soviets* of the republic which had so offended "the self-esteem of the government", was of extreme value, and essential for bringing about the "shift in the mood of the masses"; that its effect was already "making itself felt", and that now the influence of Bolshevik propaganda would "decline rapidly". On the other hand, according to Dan's own words, the Bolsheviks themselves had declared, in negotiations with the leaders of the *soviet* majority, their readiness to "submit to the will of the *soviet* majority", and that they were ready "tomorrow" to use all measures to quell the insurrection which flared up against their own wishes and without their sanction! In conclusion, after mentioning that the Bolsheviks would disband their military staff "tomorrow" (always tomorrow!) Dan declared that all the measures I had taken to crush the insurrection had only "irritated the masses" and that by my meddling I was generally "hindering the representatives of the *soviet* majority" from successfully concluding their negotiations with the Bolsheviks for the liquidation of the insurrection . . .

'To complete the picture, I ought to add that at the very moment Dan was imparting to me this remarkable information, the armed detachments of "Red Guards" were occupying government buildings, one after another. And almost immediately after the departure of Dan and his comrades from the Winter Palace, Minister Kartashev, on his way home from a session of the Provisional Government, was arrested on Milliony street and taken directly to Smolny, whither Dan was returning to resume his peaceful conversations with the Bolsheviks. I must confess that the Bolsheviks deported themselves at that time with great energy and no less skill. At the moment when the insurrection was in full blast, and while the "red troops" were operating all over the city, several Bolshevik leaders especially designated for the purpose sought, not unsuccessfully, to make the representatives of "revolutionary democracy" see but remain blind, hear but remain deaf. All night long these wily men engaged in endless squabbles over various formulas which were supposed to serve as the basis for reconciliation and for the liquidation of the insurrection. By this method of "negotiating" the Bolsheviks gained a great deal of time. But the fighting forces of the SRs and the Mensheviks were not mobilized in time. But, of course, this is *QED*!'[27]

Well put! *QED*! The conciliationists, as we gather from the above account, were completely hooked with the bait of *soviet* legality. Kerensky's assumption that certain Bolsheviks were specially disguised in order to deceive the Mensheviks and the SRs about the pending liquidation of the insurrection is in fact not true. As a matter of fact, the Bolsheviks most actively participating in the negotiations were those who really desired the liquidation of the insurrection, and who believed in the formula of a socialist government, formed by the conciliation of all parties. Objectively, however, these parliamentarians doubtless proved of some service to the insurrection—feeding, with their own illusions, the illusions of the enemy. But they were able to render this service to the revolution only because the party, in spite of all their counsels and all their warnings, pressed on with the insurrection with unabating energy and carried it through to the end.

A combination of altogether exceptional circumstances—great and small—was needed to insure the success of this extensive and enveloping maneuver. Above all, an army was needed which was unwilling to fight any longer. The entire course of the revolution—particularly during the initial stages—from February to October, inclusive, would have been, as we have already said, altogether different if at the moment of revolution there had not existed in the country a broken and discontented peasant army of many millions. These conditions alone made it possible to bring to a successful conclusion the experiment with the Petrograd garrison, which predetermined the victorious outcome of October.

There cannot be the slightest talk of sanctifying into any sort of a law this peculiar combination of a 'dry' and almost imperceptible insurrection together with the defense of *soviet* legality against Kornilov and his followers. On the contrary, we can state with certainty that this experience will never be repeated anywhere in such a form. But a careful study of it is most necessary. It will tend to broaden the horizon of every revolutionist, disclosing before him the multiplicity and variety of ways and means which can be set in motion, provided the goal is kept clearly in mind, the situation is correctly appraised, and there is a determination to carry the struggle through to the end.

In Moscow, the insurrection took much longer and entailed much greater sacrifices. The explanation for this lies partly in the fact that the Moscow garrison was not subjected to the same revolutionary preparation as the Petrograd garrison in connection with the transfer of regiments to the front. We have already said, and we repeat, that the armed insurrection in Petrograd was carried out in two installments: the first in the early part of October, when the Petrograd regiments, obeying the decision of the *soviet*, which harmonized completely with their own desires, refused to carry out the orders from headquarters—and did so with impunity—and the second on 25 October, when only a minor and supplementary insurrection was required in order to sever the umbilical cord of the February state power. But in Moscow, the insurrection took place in a single stage, and that was probably the main reason that it was so protracted.

But there was also another reason: the leadership was not decisive enough. In Moscow we saw a swing from military action to negotiations only to be followed by another swing from negotiations to military action. If vacillations on the part of the leaders, which are transmitted to the followers, are generally harmful in politics, then they become a mortal danger under the conditions of an armed insurrection. The ruling class has already lost confidence in its own strength (otherwise there could, in general, be no hope for victory) but the apparatus still remains in its hands. The task of the revolutionary class is to conquer the state apparatus. To do so, it must have confidence in its own forces. Once the party has led the workers to insurrection, it has to draw from this all the necessary conclusions. *A la guerre comme à la guerre* ('War is war'). Under war conditions, vacillation and procrastination are less permissible than at any other time. The measuring stick of war is a short one. To mark time, even for a few hours, is to restore a measure of confidence to the ruling class while taking it away from the insurgents. But this is precisely what determines the relationship of forces, which, in turn, determines the outcome of the insurrection. From this point of view it is necessary to study, step by step, the course of military operations in Moscow in their connection with the political leadership.

It would be of great significance to indicate several other instances where the civil war took place under special conditions, being complicated, for instance, by the intrusion of a national element. Such a study, based upon carefully digested factual data, would greatly enrich our knowledge of the mechanics of civil war and thereby facilitate the elaboration of certain methods, rules, and devices of a sufficiently general character to serve as a sort of 'manual' of civil war. But in anticipation of the partial conclusions of such a study, it may be said that the course of the civil war in the provinces was largely determined by the outcome in Petrograd, even despite the delay in Moscow. The February revolution cracked the old apparatus. The Provisional Government inherited it, and was unable either to renew it or to strengthen it. In consequence, its state apparatus functioned between February and October only as a relic of bureaucratic inertia. The provincial bureaucracy had become accustomed to do what Petrograd did; it did this in February, and repeated it in October. It was an enormous advantage to us that we were preparing to overthrow a regime which had not yet had time to consolidate itself. The extreme instability and want of assurance of the February state apparatus facilitated our work in the extreme by instilling the revolutionary masses and the party itself with self-assurance.

A similar situation existed in Germany and Austria after 9 November 1918. There, however, the social democracy filled in the cracks of the state apparatus and helped to establish a bourgeois republican regime; and though this regime cannot be considered a pattern of stability, it has nevertheless already survived six years.

So far as other capitalist countries are concerned, they will not have this advantage, i.e. the proximity of a bourgeois and a proletarian revolution. Their February is already long past. To be sure, in England there are a good many relics of feudalism, but there are absolutely no grounds for speaking of an independent bourgeois revolution in England. Purging the country of the monarchy, and the Lords, and the rest, will be achieved by the first sweep of the broom of the English proletariat when they come into power. The proletarian revolution in the West will have to deal with a completely established bourgeois state. But this does not mean that it will have to deal with a stable state apparatus; for the very possibility of proletarian insurrection implies an extremely advanced process of the disintegration of the capitalist state. In our country the October Revolution unfolded in the struggle with a state apparatus which did not succeed in stabilizing itself after February, then in other countries the insurrection will be confronted with a state apparatus in a state of progressive disintegration.

It may be assumed as a general rule—we pointed this out as far back as the Fourth World Congress of the Comintern*—that the force of the pre-October resistance of the bourgeoisie in old capitalist countries will generally be much greater than in our country; it will be more difficult

---

*   In November 1922.

for the proletariat to gain victory; but, on the other hand, the conquest of power will immediately secure for them a much more stable and firm position than we attained on the day after October. In our country, the civil war took on real scope only after the proletariat had conquered power in the chief cities and industrial centers, and it lasted for the first three years of *soviet* rule. There is every indication that in the countries of Central and Western Europe it will be much more difficult for the proletariat to conquer power, but that after the seizure of power they will have a much freer hand. Naturally, these considerations concerning prospects are only hypothetical. A good deal will depend on the order in which revolutions take place in the different countries of Europe, the possibilities of military intervention, the economic and military strength of the Soviet Union at the time, and so on. But in any case, our basic and, we believe, incontestable postulate—that the actual process of the conquest of power will encounter in Europe and America a much more serious, obstinate, and prepared resistance from the ruling classes than was the case with us—makes it all the more incumbent upon us to view the armed insurrection in particular and civil war in general as an art.

Chapter Eight
Again on the *soviets* and the party in a proletarian revolution

IN OUR COUNTRY, both in 1905 and in 1917, the *soviets* of workers' deputies grew out of the movement itself as its natural organizational form at a certain stage of the struggle. But the young European parties, who have more or less accepted *soviets* as a 'doctrine' and 'principle', always run the danger of treating *soviets* as a fetish, as some self-sufficing factor in a revolution. Yet, in spite of the enormous advantages of *soviets* as the organs of struggle for power, there may well be cases where the insurrection may unfold on the basis of other forms of organization (factory committees, trade unions, etc.) and *soviets* may spring up only during the insurrection itself, or even after it has achieved victory, as organs of state power.

Most highly instructive from this standpoint is the struggle which Lenin launched after the July days against the fetishism of the organizational form of *soviets*. In proportion as the SR-Menshevik *soviets* became, in July, organizations openly driving the soldiers into an offensive and crushing the Bolsheviks, to that extent the revolutionary movement of the proletarian masses was obliged and compelled to seek new paths and channels. Lenin indicated the factory committees as the organizations of the struggle for power. (See, for instance, the reminiscences of Comrade Ordzhonikidze.) It is very likely that the movement would have proceeded on those lines if it had not been for the Kornilov uprising, which forced the conciliationist *soviets* to defend themselves and made it possible for the Bolsheviks to imbue them with a new revolutionary vigor, binding them closely to the masses through the left, i.e. Bolshevik wing.

This question is of enormous international importance, as was shown by the recent German experience. It was in Germany that *soviets* were several times created as organs of insurrection—without an insurrection taking place—and as organs of state power—without any power. This led to the following: in 1923, the movement of broad proletarian and semi-proletarian masses began to crystallize around the factory committees, which *in the main* fulfilled all the functions assumed by our own *soviets* in the period preceding the direct struggle for power. Yet, during August and September 1923, several comrades advanced the proposal that we should proceed to the immediate creation of *soviets* in Germany. After a long and heated discussion this proposal was rejected, and rightly so. In view of the fact that the factory committees had already become in action the rallying centers of the revolutionary masses, *soviets* would only have been a parallel form of organization, without any real content, during the preparatory stage. They could have only distracted attention from the material targets of the insurrection (army, police, armed bands, railways, etc.) by fixing it on a self-contained organizational form.

And, on the other hand, the creation of *soviets* as such, prior to the insurrection and apart from the immediate tasks of the insurrection, would have meant an open proclamation, 'We mean to attack you!' The government, compelled to 'tolerate' the factory committees insofar as the latter had become the rallying centers of great masses, would have struck at the very first *soviet* as an official organ of an 'attempt' to seize power. The communists would have had to come out in defense of the *soviets* as purely organizational entities. The decisive struggle would have broken out not in order to seize or defend any material positions, nor at a moment chosen by us—a moment when the insurrection would flow from the conditions of the mass movement; no, the struggle would have flared up over the *soviet* 'banner', at a moment chosen by the enemy and forced upon us.

In the meantime, it is quite clear that the entire preparatory work for the insurrection could have been carried out successfully under the authority of the factory and shop committees, which were already established as mass organizations and which were constantly growing in numbers and strength; and that this would have allowed the party to maneuver freely with regard to fixing the date for the insurrection. *Soviets*, of course, would have had to arise at a certain stage. It is doubtful whether, under the above-mentioned conditions, they would have arisen as the direct organs of insurrection, in the very fire of the conflict, because of the risk of creating two revolutionary centers at the most critical moment. An English proverb says that you must not swap horses while crossing a stream. It is possible that *soviets* would have been formed after the victory at all the decisive places in the country. In any case, a triumphant insurrection would inevitably have led to the creation of *soviets* as organs of state power.

It must not be forgotten that in our country the *soviets* grew up in the 'democratic' stage of the revolution, becoming legalized, as it were, at that stage, and subsequently being inherited and utilized by us. This will not be repeated in the proletarian revolutions of the West. There, in most cases, the *soviets* will be created in response to the call of the communists; and they will consequently be created as the direct organs of proletarian insurrection. To be sure, it is not at all excluded that the disintegration of the bourgeois state apparatus will have become quite acute before the proletariat is able to seize power; this would create the conditions for the formation of *soviets as the open organs of preparing the insurrection*. But this is not likely to be the general rule. Most likely, it will be possible to create *soviets* only in the very last days, as the direct organs of the insurgent masses. Finally, it is quite probable that such circumstances will arise as will make the *soviets* emerge either after the insurrection has passed its critical stage, or even in its closing stages as organs of the new state power.

All these variants must be kept in mind so as to safeguard us from falling into organizational fetishism, and so as not to transform the *soviets* from what they ought to be—a flexible and living form of struggle—into an organizational 'principle' imposed upon the movement from the outside, disrupting its normal development.

There has been some talk lately in our press to the effect that we are not, mind you, in a position to tell through what channels the proletarian revolution will come in England. Will it come through the channel of the Communist Party or through the trade unions? Such a formulation of the question makes a show of a fictitiously broad historical outlook; it is radically false and dangerous because it obliterates the chief lesson of the last few years. If the triumphant revolution did not come at the end of the war, it was because a party was lacking. This conclusion applies to Europe as a whole. It may be traced concretely in the fate of the revolutionary movement in various countries.

With respect to Germany, the case is quite a clear one. The German revolution might have been triumphant both in 1918 and in 1919, had a proper party leadership been secured. We had an instance of this same thing in 1917 in the case of Finland. There, the revolutionary movement developed under exceptionally favorable circumstances, under the wing of revolutionary Russia and with its direct military assistance. But the majority of the leaders in the Finnish party proved to be social democrats, and they ruined the revolution. The same lesson flows just as plainly from the Hungarian experience. There the communists, along with the left social democrats, did not conquer power, but were handed it by the frightened bourgeoisie. The Hungarian revolution—triumphant without a battle and without a victory—was left from the very outset without a fighting leadership. The Communist Party fused with the social democratic party, showed thereby that it itself was not a Communist Party; and in consequence, in spite of the fighting spirit of the Hungarian workers, it proved incapable of keeping the power it had obtained so easily.

Without a party, apart from a party, over the head of a party, or with a substitute for a party, the proletarian revolution cannot conquer. That is the principal lesson of the past decade. It is true that the English trade unions may become a mighty lever of the proletarian revolution; they may, for instance, even take the place of workers' *soviets* under certain conditions and for a certain period of time. They can fill such a role, however, not apart from a Communist party, and certainly not *against* the party, but only on the condition that communist influence becomes the decisive influence in the trade unions. We have paid far too dearly for this conclusion—with regard to the role and importance of a party in a proletarian revolution—to renounce it so lightly or even to minimize its significance.

Consciousness, premeditation, and planning played a far smaller part in bourgeois revolutions than they are destined to play, and already do play, in proletarian revolutions. In the former instance the motive force of the revolution was also furnished by the masses, but the latter were much less organized and much less conscious than at the present time. The leadership remained in the hands of different sections of the bourgeoisie, and the latter had at its disposal wealth, education, and all the organizational advantages connected with them (the cities, the universities, the press, etc.). The bureaucratic monarchy defended itself in a hand-to-mouth manner, probing in the dark and then acting. The bourgeoisie would bide its time to seize a favorable moment when it could profit from the movement of the lower classes, throw its whole social weight into the scale, and so seize the state power. The proletarian revolution is precisely distinguished by the fact that the proletariat—in the person of its vanguard—acts in it not only as the main offensive force but also as the guiding force. The part played in bourgeois revolutions by the economic power of the bourgeoisie, by its education, by its municipalities and universities, is a part which can be filled in a proletarian revolution only by the party of the proletariat.

The role of the party has become all the more important in view of the fact that the enemy has also become far more conscious. The bourgeoisie, in the course of centuries of rule, has perfected a political schooling far superior to the schooling of the old bureaucratic monarchy. If parliamentarism served the proletariat to a certain extent as a training school for revolution, then it also served the bourgeoisie to a far greater extent as the school of counterrevolutionary strategy. Suffice it to say that by means of parliamentarism the bourgeoise was able so to train the social democracy that it is today the main prop of private property. The epoch of the social revolution in Europe, as has been shown by its very first steps, will be an epoch not only of strenuous and ruthless struggle but also of planned and calculated battles—far more planned than with us in 1917.

That is why we require an approach entirely different from the prevailing one to the questions of civil war in general and of armed insurrection in particular. Following Lenin, all of us keep repeating time and again Marx's words that insurrection is an art. But this idea is transformed into a hollow phrase, to the extent that Marx's formula is not supplemented with a study of the fundamental elements of the art of civil war, on the basis of the vast accumulated experience of recent years. It is necessary to say candidly that a superficial attitude to questions of armed insurrection is a token that the power of the social democratic tradition has not yet been overcome. A party which pays superficial attention to the question of civil war, in the hope that everything will somehow settle itself at the crucial moment, is certain to be shipwrecked. We must analyze in a collective manner the experience of the proletarian struggles beginning with 1917.

The above-sketched history of the party groupings in 1917 also constitutes an integral part of the experience of civil war and is, we believe, of immediate importance to the policies of the Communist International as a whole. We have already said, and we repeat, that the study of disagreements cannot, and ought not in any case, be regarded as an attack against those comrades who pursued a false policy. But on the other hand it is absolutely impermissible to blot out the greatest chapter in the history of our party merely because some party members failed to keep step with the proletarian revolution. The party should and must know the *whole* of the past, so as to be able to estimate it correctly and assign each event to its proper place. The tradition of a revolutionary party is built not on evasions but on critical clarity.

History secured for our party revolutionary advantages that are truly inestimable. The traditions of the heroic struggle against the tsarist monarchy; the habituation to revolutionary self-sacrifice bound up with the conditions of underground activity; the broad theoretical study and assimilation of the revolutionary experience of humanity; the struggle against Menshevism, against the Narodniks, and against conciliationism; the supreme experience of the 1905 revolution; the theoretical study and assimilation of this experience during the years of counter-revolution; the examination of the problems of the international labor movement in the light of the revolutionary lessons of 1905—these were the things which in their totality gave our party an exceptional revolutionary temper, supreme theoretical penetration, and unparalleled revolutionary sweep. Nevertheless, even within this party, among its leaders, on the eve of decisive action there was formed a group of experienced revolutionists, Old Bolsheviks, who were in sharp opposition to the proletarian revolution and who, in the course of the most critical period of the revolution from February 1917 to approximately February 1918, adopted on all fundamental questions an essentially social democratic position. It required Lenin, and Lenin's exceptional influence in the party, unprecedented even at that time, to safeguard the party and the revolution against the supreme confusion following from such a situation. This must never be forgotten if we wish other Communist parties to learn anything from us.

The question of selecting the leading staff is of exceptional importance to the parties of Western Europe. The experience of the abortive German October is shocking proof of this. But this selection must proceed in the light of *revolutionary action*. During these recent years, Germany has provided ample opportunities for the testing of the leading party members in moments of direct struggle. Failing this criterion, the rest is worthless. France, during these years, was much poorer in revolutionary upheavals—even partial ones.

But even in the political life of France we have had flashes of civil war, times when the Central Committee of the party and the trade union leadership had to react in action to unpostponable and acute questions (such as the sanguinary meeting of 11 January 1924). A careful study of such acute episodes provides irreplaceable material for the evaluation of a party leadership, the conduct of various party organs, and individual leading members. To ignore these lessons—not to draw the necessary conclusions from them as to the choice of personalities—is to invite inevitable defeats; for without a penetrating, resolute, and courageous party leadership, the victory of the proletarian revolution is impossible.

Each party, even the most revolutionary party, must inevitably produce its own organizational conservatism; for otherwise it would lack the necessary stability. This is wholly a question of degree. In a revolutionary party the vitally necessary dose of conservatism must be combined with a complete freedom from routine, with initiative in orientation and daring in action. These qualities are put to the severest test during turning points in history. We have already quoted the words of Lenin to the effect that even the most revolutionary parties, when an abrupt change occurs in a situation and when new tasks arise as a consequence, frequently pursue the political line of yesterday and thereby become, or threaten to become, a brake upon the revolutionary process. Both conservatism and revolutionary initiative find their most concentrated expression in the leading organs of the party. In the meantime, the European Communist parties have still to face their sharpest 'turning point'—the turn from preparatory work to the actual seizure of power. This turn is the most exacting, the most unpostponable, the most responsible, and the most formidable. To miss the moment for the turn is to incur the greatest defeat that a party can possibly suffer.

The experience of the European struggles, and above all the struggles in Germany, when looked at in the light of our own experience, tells us that there are two types of leaders who incline to drag the party back at the very moment when it must take a stupendous leap forward. Some among them generally tend to see mainly the difficulties and obstacles in the way of revolution, and to estimate each situation with a preconceived, though not always conscious, intention of avoiding any action. Marxism in their hands is turned into a method for establishing the impossibility of revolutionary action. The purest specimens of this type are the Russian Mensheviks. But this type as such is not confined to Menshevism, and at the most critical moment it suddenly manifests itself in responsible posts in the most revolutionary party.

The representatives of the second variety are distinguished by their superficial and agitational approach. They never see any obstacles or difficulties until they come into a head-on collision with them. The capacity for surmounting real obstacles by means of bombastic phrases, the tendency to evince lofty optimism on all questions ('the ocean is only knee deep'), is inevitably transformed into its polar opposite when the hour for decisive action strikes. To the first type of revolutionist, who makes mountains out of molehills, the problems of seizing power lie in heaping up and multiplying to the nth degree all the difficulties he has become accustomed to see in his way. To the second type, the superficial optimist, the difficulties of revolutionary action always come as a surprise. In the preparatory period the behavior of the two is different: the former is a skeptic upon whom one cannot rely too much, that is, in a revolutionary sense; the latter, on the contrary, may seem a fanatic revolutionist. But at the decisive moment, the two march hand in hand; they both oppose the insurrection. Meanwhile, the entire preparatory work is of value only to the extent that it renders the party and above all its leading organs capable of determining the moment for an insurrection, and of assuming the leadership of it. For the task of the Communist Party is the conquest of power for the purpose of reconstructing society.

Much has been spoken and written lately on the necessity of 'Bolshevizing' the Comintern. This is a task that cannot be disputed or delayed; it is made particularly urgent after the cruel lessons of Bulgaria and Germany a year ago. Bolshevism is not a doctrine (i.e. not merely a doctrine) but a system of revolutionary training for the proletarian uprising. What is the Bolshevization of Communist parties? It is giving them such a training, and effecting such a selection of the leading staff, as would prevent them from drifting when the hour for their October strikes. 'That is the whole of Hegel, and the wisdom of books, and the meaning of all philosophy . . . '

Suggested further reading

The most obvious point at which to follow up the issues raised here is Leon Trotsky's own *History of the Russian Revolution*. This was first published in English in 1932–33 and is available in several editions. The problems faced by the Bolsheviks both during and after the revolution are also discussed in detail in Tony Cliff's three-volume biography of Lenin, particularly the second volume: *All Power to the Soviets 1914–17*, and the third: *Revolution Besieged 1917–23*. Both are published by Bookmarks.

Those who wish to see *The Lessons of October* within the context of the political battles inside Russia should read the collection of Trotsky's writings in *The Challenge of the Left Opposition 1923–25*, which is published by Pathfinder Press in New York.

On the life and political ideas of Trotsky himself, a good short introduction is Duncan Hallas' *Trotsky's Marxism*, published by Bookmarks in 1979, while Isaac Deutscher's three-volume biography—*The Prophet Armed 1879–1921*, *The Prophet Unarmed 1921–29* and *The Prophet Outcast 1929–40*—is unrivalled. It is published by the Oxford University Press.

Trotsky touches on three other topics of which readers may wish to learn more. On Germany, read Chris Harman's *The Lost Revolution: Germany 1918–23* (Bookmarks 1982); on the Russian working-class upsurge before 1914, read *Bolsheviks in the Tsarist Duma* by A Y Badayev (Bookmarks 1987); and on the development and degeneration of the international communist movement after 1919 read Duncan Hallas' *The Comintern* (Bookmarks 1985).*

---

* Several of the books mentioned have since been reprinted by Haymarket Books: *History of the Russian Revolution* [2008 and 2017], *All Power to the Soviets* [2004], *The Revolution Besieged* [2012], *The Lost Revolution* [2008 and 2017] and *The Comintern* [2008].

References

Notes to Introduction

1. E H Carr, *Socialism in One Country* (London 1972) volume 2, page 19.
2. Isaac Deutscher, *Trotsky: The Prophet Unarmed* (London 1959) page 154.
3. Deutscher, page 9.

Notes to text

1. V I Lenin, *Collected Works*, volume 25 (Moscow 1964) page 183. Lenin was writing in July 1917.
2. F Engels, *The Peasant War in Germany* (Moscow 1965) page 13.
3. Lenin, volume 24 (Moscow 1964) pages 44–50, writing in April 1917.
4. *Pravda*, number 9, 15 March 1917.
5. *Pravda*, number 9, 15 March 1917.
6. *Pravda*, number 10, 16 March 1917.
7. Lenin, volume 23 (Moscow 1964) pages 315–336.

8. Lenin, 'The tasks of the proletariat in the present revolution', 4 April 1917, in *Collected Works*, volume 24, page 22.
9. Lenin, 'Tasks of the proletariat in our revolution—a draft programme for the proletarian party', 28 May 1917, in *Collected Works*, volume 24, page 76.
10. Lenin, volume 25, page 204.
11. Lenin, volume 25, pages 240–1.
12. Lenin, volume 24, page 88.
13. Lenin, volume 25, pages 285–6.
14. Lenin, volume 26, page 48.
15. Lenin, volume 26, page 25.
16. Lenin, volume 26, page 84.
17. *Novaya Zhizn*, number 156, 18 October 1917.
18. 'The October Revolution' in *Archives of the Revolution 1917*, pages 407–10.
19. 'The October Revolution' in *Archives of the Revolution 1917*, pages 407–10.
20. *Rabochaya Gazeta* (Workers' Gazette), number 204, 5 November 1917.
21. Lenin, volume 26, pages 305–6.
22. Lenin, 'Marxism and Insurrection', 13–14 September 1917, in *Collected Works*, volume 26, page 27.
23. Lenin, volume 26, page 82.
24. Lenin, volume 26, page 141.
25. Lenin, volume 26, page 144.
26. Lenin, volume 26, pages 234–5.
27. A Kerensky, *From Afar*, pages 197–8.

Appendix I:

Events in Russia 1917

16 February: Mass working-class demonstrations protest in Petrograd over food shortages resulting from the war.

23 February: Mass protests and marches for International Women's Day begin the February revolution.

26 February: State Duma (parliament) dissolved by the Tsar.

27 February: Mutiny of Guards regiments. Formation of Petrograd Soviet.

28 February: Tsar's ministers arrested.

2 March: The Tsar abdicates. Formation of the Provisional Government with support of the Soviet and Kerensky as Minister of Justice.

5 March: First issue of Bolshevik paper *Pravda*.

14 March: Address of Soviet 'to the peoples of the whole world'.

3 April: Lenin reaches Petrograd from Switzerland.

4 April: Lenin's *April Theses* outline his policy of proletarian revolution.

18 April: Miliukov, on behalf of Provisional Government, promises allies 'war to victory'.

19 April: Armed protest demonstrations against Miliukov's action.

24–29 April: April Conference of Bolsheviks.

4 May: Trotsky arrives in Petrograd from America.

3 June: First All-Russian Congress of Soviets.

3–4 July: The July Days, mass demonstrations in Petrograd against the Provisional Government.

5–7 July: Arrest of Bolshevik leaders ordered; Lenin goes into hiding.

23 July: Trotsky arrested.

August–September: Lenin writes *State and Revolution*.

27–30 August: Attempted coup by General Kornilov defeated by armed workers, mobilised by Bolsheviks.

1 September: Petrograd Soviet carries a Bolshevik motion.

9 September: Leaders of the Petrograd Soviet go over to Bolsheviks.

15 September: Bolshevik central committee discusses Lenin's letters calling for insurrection.

5 October: Kerensky orders despatch of troops from Petrograd to the front.

7 October: Opening of 'Pre-Parliament'; Bolsheviks refuse to take part.

9 October: Formation of Military Revolutionary Committee of Petrograd Soviet; it co-ordinates resistance to the movement of troops.

10 October: Bolshevik central committee declares for armed insurrection.

16 October: Plenum of Bolsheviks in Petrograd reaffirms decision on insurrection.

18 October: Publication of letter by Kamenev and Zinoviev opposing insurrection.

24 October: Provisional Government orders arrest of Military Revolutionary Committee.

25 October: 2am: Insurrection. *9pm:* Occupation of Winter Palace, seat of Provisional Government. *11pm:* Opening of Second All-Russian Congress of Soviets.

Appendix 2:

Events in Germany 1923

January: Local elections in Bulgaria give Peasant Union 437,000 votes and Communist Party 230,000, while the bourgeois parties together receive only 220,000.

January: French forces occupy the German Ruhr demanding 'war reparations', precipitating political crisis in Germany.

April: General election of Peasant Union government in Bulgaria led by Stambulisky.

April: Hyper-inflation hits Germany, rendering the currency worthless and sparking waves of unofficial strikes during May, June and July with the setting up of workers' militia as a defence against the right.

June: Membership of the German Communist Party reaches 70,000.

9 June: Bulgarian army and police, backed by right-wing political parties, launch coup against Peasant Union government. Communist Party, which has 39,000 members, stands aside from what it calls 'a struggle between two wings of the capitalist class'. Military regime established under Tsankov.

12 June: Executive of Communist International calls on Bulgarian Communist Party to ally with the peasantry in common struggle against the right.

29 July: German Anti-Fascist Day of demonstrations, planned by Communist Party, called off as party leadership loses its nerve in face of growing mass struggle.

11 August: Second wave of strikes in Germany. Berlin delegates of factory councils call for immediate general strike to bring down Cuno government. Cuno resigns in favour of coalition of social democrats and bourgeois parties.

August: Bulgarian Communist Party, facing repression from military regime, acts on the advice of Zinoviev as leader of the Communist International and plans armed rising for 22 September, despite disorganisation and demoralisation of workers and peasants. In Germany an insurrection is also planned, but there it is on a rising wave of working-class struggle.

September: Tsankov, hearing of planned Bulgarian insurrection, orders mass arrests. Scattered, unco-ordinated risings are viciously suppressed.

20 October: German army moves into province of Saxony to suppress left-wing Social Democratic provincial government. When Social Democrats fail to respond to call for armed resistance and general strike, Communist Party leadership backs down and calls off planned insurrection.

22 October: Message calling off rising fails to reach Hamburg, where the local Communists stage insurrection. Isolated, they are crushed by government troops.

Also from Haymarket Books

Lessons of October
Leon Trotsky

**History of the
Russian Revolution**
Leon Trotsky

The Bolsheviks Come to Power
Alexander Rabinowitch

Reminiscences of Lenin
Nadezhda K. Krupskaya

Trotsky on Lenin
Leon Trotsky

Lenin's Moscow
Alfred Rosmer,
Translated by Ian Birchall

**The Life and Death
of Leon Trotsky**
Natalia Sedova and Victor Serge

**Lenin and the
Revolutionary Party**
Paul Le Blanc

**Year One of the
Russian Revolution**
Victor Serge

State and Revolution
V.I. Lenin
Edited by Todd Chretien

**Leon Trotsky and the
Organizational Principles
of the Revolutionary Party**
Dianne Feeley, Paul Le Blanc and
Thomas Twiss
Introduction by George Breitman

Unfinished Leninism
Paul Le Blanc

Leon Trotsky
An Illustrated Introduction
Tariq Ali, Illustrated by Phil Evans

Revolution in Danger
Victor Serge

**Revolution and
Counterrevolution**
Class Struggle in a
Moscow Metal Factory
Kevin Murphy

Building the Party
Lenin 1893–1914 (Vol. 1)
Tony Cliff

In Celebration of the Centenary
of the Russian Revolution

All Power to the Soviets
Lenin 1914–1917 (Vol. 2)
Tony Cliff

The Revolution Besieged
Lenin 1917–1923 (Vol. 3)
Tony Cliff

Russia
From Workers' State
to State Capitalism
Anthony Arnove, Tony Cliff,
Chris Harman and Ahmed Shawki

Lenin's Political Thought
Neil Harding

Alexandra Kollontai
A Biography
Cathy Porter

Clara Zetkin
Selected Writings
Clara Zetkin, Edited by Philip S. Foner,
Foreword by Angela Y. Davis
and Rosalyn Baxandall

1905
Leon Trotsky

**Alexander Shlyapnikov,
1885–1937**
Barbara C. Allen

**The October Revolution in
Prospect and Retrospect**
John E. Marot

**The Russian Social-
Democratic Labour Party
1889–1904**
Edited by Richard Mullin

Lenin Rediscovered
Lars T. Lih

To the Masses
Proceedings of the Third Congress of
the Communist International, 1921
Edited by John Riddell

Toward the United Front
Proceedings of the Fourth Congress
of the Communist International, 1922
Edited by John Riddell

**Trotsky and the Problem
of Soviet Bureaucracy**
Thomas Twiss